Polycarp, Papias, and Diognetus

APOSTOLIC FATHERS GREEK READER

VOLUME 3

Polycarp, Papias, and Diognetus

APOSTOLIC FATHERS GREEK READER

VOLUME 3

EDITED BY
Shawn J. Wilhite and Jacob N. Cerone

INTRODUCTIONS BY
Michael A. G. Haykin
Shawn J. Wilhite

NOTES BY
Michael T. Graham Jr. (Polycarp's Epistle to the Philippians)
Shawn J. Wilhite (Martyrdom of Polycarp)
Matthew McMains (Papias)
Matthew Albanese (Diognetus)

GlossaHouse   G*H*
Wilmore, KY
www.glossahouse.com

Polycarp, Papias, and Diognetus
© GlossaHouse, LLC, 2018

GlossaHouse, LLC 110 Callis Circle Wilmore, KY 40309

www.GlossaHouse.com

Publisher's Cataloging-in-Publication Data

Polycarp, Papias, and Diognetus. Greek.

Polycarp, Papias, and Diognetus / edited by Shawn J. Wilhite and Jacob N. Cerone; introductions by Michael A.G. Haykin and Shawn J. Wilhite; notes by Michael T. Graham Jr. (Polycarp's Epistle to the Philippians), Shawn J. Wilhite (Martyrdom of Polycarp), Matthew McMains (Papias), and Matthew Albanese (Diognetus). – Wilmore, KY : GlossaHouse, ©2018.

xvi, 109 pages ; 22 cm. -- (AGROS) -- (Apostolic fathers Greek reader ; vol. 3)

Greek text of Polycarp, Papias, and Diognetus, accompanied by the English translation of many select words in footnotes. Includes bibliographical references.

ISBN: 978-1942697749 (paperback)

1. Polycarp's Epistle to the Philippians—Introductions. 2. Christian ethics—History—Early church, ca. 30-600. 3. Church—History of doctrines—Early church, ca. 30-600. 4. Martyrdom of Polycarp. 5. Papias—Introductions. 5. Diognetus to Mathetes I. Title. II. Apostolic fathers Greek reader; vol. 3. III. Accessible Greek resources and online studies. IV. Polycarp. Greek. V. Papias. Greek VI. Diognetus to Mathetes. Greek. VII. Wilhite, Shawn J. VIII. Cerone, Jacob N. IX. Haykin, Michael A. G. X. Anderson, Jason.

Library of Congress Control Number: 2018955128

The fonts used to create this work are available from linguistsoftware.com/lgku.htm.

Cover design by T. Michael W. Halcomb.

Text layout by Jacob N. Cerone.

Greek text of Polycarp's Epistle to the Philippians, Papias, and Diognetus is from J. B. Lightfoot's text (London: Macmillan, 1881) and the Martyrdom of Polycarp is from Kirsopp Lake *The Apostolic Fathers* (Cambridge: Harvard University Press, 1912–1913); to these have been added footnotes with parsing helps and brief English glosses. Includes bibliographical references.

This series is dedicated to all who have struggled to make Greek a regular part of their study of Scripture.

CONTENTS

Series Introductions
    The AGROS Series   viii
    Apostolic Fathers Greek Readers Series   x

Acknowledgments   xiii
A Note about the Apostolic Fathers Greek Reader   xiv
Abbreviations   xvi

Introduction to Polycarp   2
Polycarp to the Philippians   5
Martyrdom of Polycarp   14

Introduction to Papias   39
Papias   46

Introduction to Diognetus   66
Diognetus   70

Additional Resources   97

AGROS

ACCESSIBLE GREEK RESOURCES AND ONLINE STUDIES

SERIES EDITORS

T. MICHAEL W. HALCOMB
FREDRICK J. LONG

VOLUME EDITOR

JACOB N. CERONE

GlossaHouse 𝒢ℋ
Wilmore, KY
www.glossahouse.com

AGROS

The Greek term ἀγρός is a field where seeds are planted and growth occurs. It also can denote a small village or community that forms around such a field. The type of community envisioned here is one that attends to Holy Scripture, particularly one that encourages the use of biblical Greek. Accessible Greek Resources and Online Studies (AGROS) is a tiered curriculum suite featuring innovative readers, grammars, specialized studies, and other exegetical resources to encourage and foster the exegetical use of biblical Greek. The goal of AGROS is to facilitate the creation and publication of innovative, accessible, and affordable print and digital resources for the exposition of Scripture within the context of the global church. The AGROS curriculum includes five tiers, and each tier is indicated on the book's cover: Tier 1 (Beginning I), Tier 2 (Beginning II), Tier 3 (Intermediate I), Tier 4 (Intermediate II), and Tier 5 (Advanced). There are also two resource tracks: Conversational and Translational. Both involve intensive study of morphology, grammar, syntax, and discourse features. The conversational track specifically values the spoken word, and the enhanced learning associated with speaking a language in actual conversation. The translational track values the written word, and encourages analytical study to aide in understanding and translating biblical Greek and other Greek literature. The two resource tracks complement one another and can be pursued independently or together.

APOSTOLIC FATHERS GREEK READERS

The Apostolic Fathers are generally assigned by historians of ancient Christianity to a narrow collection of non-canonical Christian texts that date within the first and second centuries AD. This brief collection includes the letters of Clement of Rome, Ignatius of Antioch, Polycarp *To the Philippians* and *The Martyrdom of Polycarp*, the Didache, Epistle of Barnabas, the Shepherd of Hermas, Diognetus, Fragments of Papias, and the fragment of Quadratus.

The goal of the APOSTOLIC FATHERS GREEK READER (AFGR) is to assist readers of ancient Christian literature. Each volume will provide unique and unfamiliar vocabulary for beginning students of the Greek language: words appearing 30 times or less in the NT. The AFGR is a Tier 4 Resource within the AGROS Series (Accessible Greek Resources and Online Studies) produced by Glossa-House.

The beckoning call of Stephen Neill and Tom Wright, in *The Interpretation of the New Testament* 1861–1986 (1988) undergirds the need for this series. Familiarity with these texts informs students of the New Testament and Church History regarding the birth of the Christian Church. "If I had my way," invites Neill and Wright, "at least five hundred pages of Lightfoot's Apostolic Fathers would be required reading for every theological student in his first year" (61). Although the AFGR is not an introduction like Lightfoot's, it nevertheless invites readers to encounter firsthand the texts of the Apostolic Fathers, thus preparing them to explore nascent Christianity.

No substitute exists for gaining mastery of reading the Greek language outside of sustained interaction with primary texts. The AFGR, we believe, will aid and encourage students and teachers to achieve this goal.

AFGR Volumes

The Letters of Ignatius Vol. 1
> — Notes by Coleman M. Ford, Robert A. van Dalen, Aaron S. Rothermel, Griffin T. Gulledge, Brian W. Davidson, Jacob N. Cerone, and Trey Moss

The Didache and Barnabas Vol. 2
> — Notes by Shawn J. Wilhite and Madison N. Pierce

Polycarp, Papias, and Diognetus Vol. 3
> — Notes by Shawn J. Wilhite, Michael T. Graham, Jr., Matthew J. Albanese, and Matthew J. McMains

1–2 Clement Vol. 4
> — Notes by Jacob N. Cerone and Jason Andersen

The Shepherd of Hermas Vol. 5
> — Notes by Adam Smith, Wyatt A. Graham, and Nathan G. Sundt

ACKNOWLEDGEMENTS

During the entire process of this project, many people deserve to be mentioned because of their help, encouragement, criticisms, and editorial eyes—especially Jonathan Pennington and Rick Brannan. Jason Fowler, in particular, helped cultivate the initial vision of the project.

Each contributor and editor deserves recognition for their diligence in the project—Matthew Albanese, Jason Anderson, Jacob Cerone, Roberto van Dalen, Brian Davidson, Coleman Ford, Michael Graham, Griffin Gulledge, Matthew McMains, Trey Moss, Madison Pierce, Aaron Rothermel, and Nathan Sundt. Paul Cable helped with the initial work on the Shepherd of Hermas. Jacob Cerone needs to be singled out for his exceptional work. He went above the expected duties by editing the Didache and Martyrdom of Polycarp. Furthermore, as the project was losing steam, he stepped in to revive it and see it to its completion. Additionally, Nathaniel Cooley helped typeset this project.

Michael Haykin, who is both mentor and friend, wrote the introduction to each book within the collection. Paul Smythe, professor at Gateway Baptist Theological Seminary, provided a list of bibliographic resources for those desiring further study in the Apostolic Fathers.

I offer special thanks to the kind folks at GlossaHouse, namely Fredrick J. Long and T. Michael W. Halcomb. Their vision for language resources has influenced this project in many beneficial ways. I am grateful for their vision for the AFGR project, their patience in its production, and their desire for accessible ancient language resources. Brian Renshaw compiled texts, vocabulary lists, and devoted countless hours to helping with this project in its initial stages.

Shawn J. Wilhite
Editor of the AFGR Series

A NOTE ABOUT THE *AFGR*

We have limited the vocabulary to those words appearing in the New Testament 30 times or less—provided via Accordance Bible Software. In this way, second year Greek students are able to make use of the Greek reader. This is an arbitrary number and a first year Greek student can make this a personal goal.

All glosses are taken from the following works and in the following order. The glosses are, at times, not contextually determined.

1. Bauer, Walter, Frederick W. Danker, William F. Arndt, and F. Wilbur Gingrich, *A Greek-English Lexicon of the New Testament and Other Early Christian Literature*. 3rd ed. Chicago: University of Chicago Press, 2000. (BDAG)

2. Henry George Liddell and Robert Scott, *A Greek-English Lexicon*. 9th ed. with new supplement. Revised by Henry Stuard Jones and Roderick McKenzie. Oxford: Oxford University Press, 1996. (LSJ)

3. G. W. H. Lampe. *A Patristic Greek Lexicon*. Oxford: Oxford University Press, 1961.

Each entry will contain the following:

1. **Nouns:** Nominative form, Genitive ending, Article, and Gloss.

   E.g. Βάσανος, ου, ἡ, torture

2. **Adjectives:**
   (a)   2nd Declension Masculine form, 1st Decl. Fem. ending, 2nd Decl. Neuter ending, Gloss.

   E.g. ψυχρός, ά, όν, cold (lit.), without enthusiasm.

(b)   3rd Declension m/f form, 3rd Decl. Neuter ending, Gloss.

E.g. ἀσεβής, ές, impious, ungodly

3.   **Verbs:**

(a) For the Indicative, Subjunctive, or Optative Mood: Lexical Entry, Verbal Form, Mood, Voice, Person, Number, Gloss.

E.g. ἀποδημέω pres act ind 3p, absent

(b) For Infinitives: Lexical Entry, Form, Voice, Mood, Gloss.

E.g. γρύζω aor act inf, mutter, complain

(c) For Participles: Lexical Entry, Form, Voice, Mood, Gender, Number, Case, Gloss.

E.g. παροικέω pres act ptcp f.s.nom., inhabit a place as a foreigner, be a stranger

This Greek reader is not designed to supplement rigorous lexical studies. Students are still encouraged to reference the aforementioned lexicons. The Greek reader intends to aid reading and permit readers to translate quickly with minimal effort.

ABBREVIATIONS

1—1st person

2—2nd person

3—3rd person

acc—accusative

act—active

adv—adverb

aor—aorist

comp—comparative

conj—conjuction

dat—dative

f—feminine

fut—future

gen—genitive

impr—improper

imp—imperfect

impv—imperative

inf—infinitive

intj—interjection

lit—literally

m—masculine

mid—middle

n—neuter

nom—nominative

opt—optative

p—plural

part—particle

pass—passive

perf—perfect

plupf—pluperfect

prep—preposition

pres—present

ptcp—participle

s—singular

sub—subjunctive

subst—substantive

superl—superlative

trans—translation

Polycarp

APOSTOLIC FATHERS GREEK READER

POLYCARP

AN INTRODUCTION

Charles E. Hill has recently reiterated the statement of Helmut Koester that Polycarp of Smyrna is "doubtlessly the most significant ecclesiastical leader of the first half" of the second century AD.[1] The letter by the martyr Ignatius to him would have made his name known throughout the eastern Mediterranean, since collections of Ignatius's letters circulated widely. And in the account of his martyrdom, he is described by his pagan persecutors as "the teacher of Asia, the father of the Christians, the destroyer of our gods."[2]

Now, in the long history of reflection upon the witness of the Ancient Church, Polycarp has been mostly cited for his sterling witness to Christ, sealed in the gift of martyrdom, and not so much for his ability as a theologian. Yet, in recent days there has been a growing appreciation of his one extant letter: what it tells us about the second-century development of the New Testament canon, the reception of the ethical admonitions of the Apostolic household tables, an early second-century understanding of the nature of Christian righteousness, and its response to theological error. On the surface, the letter looks fairly simple. Yet, like the Johannine epistles, there are hidden riches and challenges, and, according to Irenaeus of Lyons, Polycarp is to be located within the Johannine community.

---

[1] *From the Lost Teaching of Polycarp: Identifying Irenaeus' Apostolic Presbyter and the Author of* Ad Diognetum, WUNT 186 (Tübingen: Mohr Siebeck, 2006), 1.

[2] Mart. Pol. 12.2.

While Martyrdom of Polycarp is a witness to many of the details of the actual death of Polycarp, there are some problematic elements. For example, consider both the smell of Polycarp's body as it was being burned and the appearance of the dove during Polycarp's martyrdom (Mart. Pol. 15–16). And yet, in both of these events, as well as in the rest of the document, what we have in addition to historical detail, is an important early attempt to frame a theology of persecution and martyrdom. Polycarp's death helped then-contemporary congregations to understand the meaning of suffering and dying for Christ.

This second-century text details three different martyrdom accounts. It praises the nobility of Germanicus, who fought with wild beasts and encouraged the "God-fearing race of Christians" through his death (Mart. Pol. 3.1–2). It discourages the concept of voluntary martyrdom as Quintus "turned coward" when he saw the wild beasts. Such voluntary pursuit of martyrdom does not evoke praise from fellow sisters and brothers because the "gospel does not teach this" (Mart. Pol. 4).

The narrative details the "blessed Polycarp" and his noble death (Mart. Pol. 1.1). These events aim to demonstrate how the "Lord might show us once again a martyrdom that is in accord with the Gospel" (Mart. Pol. 1.1). So, the narrative models for the reader a martyrdom that is worthy of imitation as it is patterned after "the Gospel."[1]

---

[1] Michael W. Holmes, "The Martyrdom of Polycarp and the New Testament Passion Narratives," in *Trajectories Through the New Testament and the Apostolic Fathers*, ed. Andrew F. Gregory and Christopher M. Tuckett (Oxford: Oxford University Press, 2005), 407–32; Paul Hartog, "The Christology of the *Martyrdom of Polycarp*: Martyrdom as Both Imitation of Christ and Election by Christ," *Perichoresis* 12. 2 (2014): 137–51; Shawn J. Wilhite, "'That We Too Might Be Imitators of Him': The *Martyrdom of Polycarp* as *Imitatio Christi*," *Churchman* 129.4 (Winter 2015): 319–36.

ΠΟΛΥΚΑΡΠΟΣ

In both of these documents, we have a valuable witness to post-New Testament theological reflection before the rise of such remarkable theologians as Irenaeus (himself a pupil of Polycarp) and Tertulllian.

Michael A. G. Haykin

ΠΟΛΥΚΑΡΠΟΥ ΕΠΙΣΤΟΛΗ
ΠΡΟΣ ΦΙΛΙΠΠΗΣΙΟΥΣ

NOTES BY MICHAEL GRAHAM

ΠΟΛΥΚΑΡΠΟΣ[1] καὶ οἱ σὺν αὐτῷ πρεσβύτεροι τῇ ἐκκλησίᾳ τοῦ Θεοῦ τῇ παροικούσῃ[2] Φιλίππους·[3] ἔλεος[4] ὑμῖν καὶ εἰρήνη παρὰ Θεοῦ παντοκράτορος[5] καὶ Ἰησοῦ Χριστοῦ τοῦ σωτῆρος[6] ἡμῶν πληθυνθείη.[7]

1:1 Συνεχάρην[8] ὑμῖν μεγάλως[9] ἐν τῷ Κυρίῳ ἡμῶν Ἰησοῦ Χριστῷ, δεξαμένοις τὰ μιμήματα[10] τῆς ἀληθοῦς[11] ἀγάπης καὶ προπέμψασιν,[12] ὡς ἐπέβαλεν[13] ὑμῖν, τοὺς ἐνειλημένους[14] τοῖς ἁγιοπρεπέσιν[15] δεσμοῖς,[16] ἅτινά ἐστιν διαδήματα[17] τῶν ἀληθῶς[18] ὑπὸ Θεοῦ καὶ τοῦ Κυρίου ἡμῶν ἐκλελεγμένων.[19] **2** καὶ ὅτι ἡ βεβαία[20] τῆς πίστεως ὑμῶν ῥίζα[21] ἐξ ἀρχαίων[22]

---

[1] Πολύκαρπος, ου, ὁ, Polycarp
[2] παροικεω pres act ptcp f.s.dat., inhabit a place as a foreigner, be a stranger
[3] Φιλιπποι, ων, οἱ, Philippi
[4] ἔλεος, ους, τό, mercy, compassion
[5] παντοκράτωρ, ορος, ὁ, almighty, omnipotent (one)
[6] σωτηρ, ηρος, ὁ, savior, deliverer
[7] πληθύνω aor pass opt 3s, increase, grow, multiply
[8] συγχαίρω aor pass ind 1s, rejoice with
[9] μεγάλως, adv, greatly
[10] μίμημα, ατος, τό, copy, image
[11] αληθής, ές, true
[12] προπέμπω aor act ptcp m.p.dat., assist someone in making a journey

[13] ἐπιβάλλω aor act ind 3s, lay on, put on
[14] ἐνειλέω perf mid/pass ptcp m.p.acc., wrap up in
[15] ἁγιοπρεπής, ές, fitting, proper, holy
[16] δεσμός, ου, ὁ, bond, fetter
[17] διάδημα, ατος, τό, royal headband, crown
[18] ἀληθῶς, adv, truly
[19] ἐκλέγομαι perf mid/pass ptcp m.p.gen., choose, select
[20] βέβαιος, α, ον, reliable, abiding
[21] ῥίζα, ης, ἡ, root
[22] ἀρχαῖος, αία, αῖον, from the beginning

5

καταγγελλομένη¹ χρόνων, μέχρι² νῦν διαμένει³ καὶ καρποφορεῖ⁴ εἰς τὸν Κύριον ἡμῶν Ἰησοῦν Χριστόν, ὃς ὑπέμεινεν⁵ ὑπὲρ τῶν ἁμαρτιῶν ἡμῶν ἕως θανάτου καταντῆσαι⁶ ὃν ἤγειρεν ὁ Θεός, λύσας τὰς ὠδῖνας⁷ τοῦ ᾅδου.⁸ **3** εἰς ὃν οὐκ ἰδόντες πιστεύετε χαρᾷ ἀνεκλαλήτῳ⁹ καὶ δεδοξασμένῃ εἰς ἣν πολλοὶ ἐπιθυμοῦσιν¹⁰ εἰσελθεῖν, εἰδότες ὅτι χάριτι ἐστε σεσωσμένοι, οὐκ ἐξ ἔργων, ἀλλὰ θελήματι Θεοῦ διὰ Ἰησοῦ Χριστοῦ.

2:1 Διὸ ἀναζωσάμενοι¹¹ τὰς ὀσφύας¹² δουλεύσατε¹³ τῷ Θεῷ ἐν φόβῳ καὶ ἀληθείᾳ, ἀπολιπόντες¹⁴ τὴν κενὴν¹⁵ ματαιολογίαν¹⁶ καὶ τὴν τῶν πολλῶν πλάνην¹⁷ πιστεύσαντες εἰς τὸν ἐγείραντα τὸν Κύριον ἡμῶν Ἰησοῦν Χριστὸν ἐκ νεκρῶν καὶ δόντα αὐτῷ δόξαν καὶ θρόνον ἐκ δεξιῶν αὐτοῦ· ᾧ ὑπετάγη τὰ πάντα ἐπουράνια¹⁸ καὶ ἐπίγεια¹⁹ ᾧ πᾶσα πνοὴ²⁰ λατρεύει,²¹ ὃς ἔρχεται κριτὴς²² ζώντων καὶ νεκρῶν, οὗ τὸ αἷμα ἐκζητήσει²³ ὁ Θεὸς ἀπὸ τῶν ἀπειθούντων²⁴ αὐτῷ. **2** ὁ δὲ ἐγείρας αὐτὸν ἐκ νεκρῶν καὶ ἡμᾶς ἐγερεῖ, ἐὰν ποιῶμεν αὐτοῦ τὸ θέλημα καὶ πορευώμεθα ἐν ταῖς ἐντολαῖς αὐτοῦ καὶ ἀγαπῶμεν ἃ ἠγάπησεν, ἀπεχόμενοι²⁵

---

¹ καταγγέλλω pres mid/pass ptcp f.s.nom., proclaim, announce
² μέχρι, adv, until
³ διαμένω pres act ind 3s, remain
⁴ καρποφορέω pres act ind 3s, bear fruit
⁵ ὑπομένω aor act ind 3s, endure, remain
⁶ καταντάω aor act inf, meet
⁷ ὠδίν, ῖνος, ἡ, great pain, birth-pain
⁸ ᾅδης, ου, ὁ, Hades
⁹ ἀνεκλάλητος, ον, inexpressible
¹⁰ ἐπιθυμέω pres act ind 3p, desire
¹¹ ἀναζώννυμι aor mid ptcp m.p.nom., bind up, gird up
¹² ὀσφύς, ύος, ἡ, loins, waist
¹³ δουλεύω aor act impv 2p, be a slave, serve, obey

¹⁴ ἀπολείπω aor act ptcp m.p.nom., put aside, give up
¹⁵ κενός, ή, όν, empty
¹⁶ ματαιολογία, ας, ἡ, empty, fruitless talk
¹⁷ πλάνη, ης, ἡ, error
¹⁸ ἐπουράνιος, ον, heavenly
¹⁹ ἐπίγειος, ον, earthly
²⁰ πνοή, ῆς, ἡ, wind, breath
²¹ λατρεύω pres act ind 3s, serve
²² κριτής, οῦ, ὁ, a judge
²³ ἐκζητέω fut act ind 3s, look for, seek
²⁴ ἀπειθέω pres act ptcp m.p.gen., disobey
²⁵ ἀπέχω pres mid/pass ptcp m.p.nom., avoid, abstain

πάσης ἀδικίας,[1] πλεονεξίας,[2] φιλαργυρίας,[3] καταλαλιάς,[4] ψευδομαρτυρίας·[5] μὴ ἀποδιδόντες κακὸν ἀντὶ[6] κακοῦ ἢ λοιδορίαν[7] ἀντὶ[8] λοιδορίας[9] ἢ γρόνθον[10] ἀντὶ[11] γρόνθου[12] ἢ κατάραν[13] ἀντὶ[14] κατάρας,[15] **3** μνημονεύοντες[16] δὲ ὧν εἶπεν ὁ Κύριος διδάσκων· μὴ κρίνετε, ἵνα μὴ κριθῆτε· ἀφίετε, καὶ ἀφεθήσεται ὑμῖν· ἐλεᾶτε[17] ἵνα ἐλεηθῆτε·[18] ᾧ μέτρῳ[19] μετρεῖτε,[20] ἀντιμετρηθήσεται[21] ὑμῖν· καὶ ὅτι μακάριοι οἱ πτωχοὶ καὶ οἱ διωκόμενοι ἕνεκεν[22] δικαιοσύνης, ὅτι αὐτῶν ἐστιν ἡ βασιλεία τοῦ Θεοῦ.

3:1 Ταῦτα, ἀδελφοί, οὐκ ἐμαυτῷ ἐπιτρέψας[23] γράφω ὑμῖν περὶ τῆς δικαιοσύνης ἀλλ' ἐπεὶ[24] ὑμεῖς προεπεκαλέσασθέ[25] με. **2** οὔτε γὰρ ἐγὼ οὔτε ἄλλος ὅμοιος ἐμοὶ δύναται κατακολουθῆσαι[26] τῇ σοφίᾳ τοῦ μακαρίου καὶ ἐνδόξου[27] Παύλου, ὃς γενόμενος ἐν ὑμῖν κατὰ πρόσωπον τῶν τότε ἀνθρώπων, ἐδίδαξεν ἀκριβῶς[28] καὶ βεβαίως[29] τὸν περὶ ἀληθείας λόγον, ὃς καὶ ἀπὼν[30]

---

[1] ἀδικία, ας, ἡ, unrighteousness
[2] πλεονεξία, ας, ἡ, covetousness
[3] φιλαργυρία, ας, ἡ, avarice, love of money
[4] καταλαλιά, ᾶς, ἡ, evil speech, slander
[5] ψευδομαρτυρία, ας, ἡ, false witness
[6] ἀντί, prep, for, instead of
[7] λοιδορία, ας, ἡ, reproach, reviling
[8] ἀντί, prep, for, instead of
[9] λοιδορία, ας, ἡ, reproach, reviling
[10] γρόνθος, ου, ὁ, blow, fist
[11] ἀντί, prep, for, instead of
[12] γρόνθος, ου, ὁ, blow, fist
[13] κατάρα, ας, ἡ, curse
[14] ἀντί, prep, for, instead of
[15] κατάρα, ας, ἡ, curse
[16] μνημονεύω pres act ptcp m.p.nom., remember
[17] ἐλεάω pres act impv 2p, have mercy
[18] ἐλεάω aor pass sub 2p, have mercy
[19] μέτρον, ου, τό, measure
[20] μετρέω pres act ind 2p, measure
[21] ἀντιμετρέω fut pass ind 3s, measure in return
[22] ἕνεκα, prep, because of, on account of
[23] ἐπιτρέπω aor act ptcp m.s.nom., to allow, permit
[24] ἐπεί, conj, since
[25] προεπικαλέω aor mid ind 2p, request
[26] κατακολουθέω aor act inf, follow
[27] ἔνδοξος, ον, honored
[28] ἀκριβῶς, adv, accurately
[29] βεβαίως, adv, reliably
[30] ἄπειμι pres act ptcp m.s.nom., be absent

ὑμῖν ἔγραψεν ἐπιστολάς· εἰς ἃς ἐὰν ἐγκύπτητε,[1] δυνηθήσεσθε οἰκοδομεῖσθαι εἰς τὴν δοθεῖσαν ὑμῖν πίστιν, **3** ἥτις ἐστὶν μήτηρ πάντων ἡμῶν, ἐπακολουθούσης[2] τῆς ἐλπίδος, προαγούσης[3] τῆς ἀγάπης τῆς εἰς Θεὸν καὶ Χριστὸν καὶ εἰς τὸν πλησίον.[4] ἐὰν γάρ τις τούτων ἐντός[5] ᾖ, πεπλήρωκεν ἐντολὴν δικαιοσύνης· ὁ γὰρ ἔχων ἀγάπην μακράν[6] ἐστιν πάσης ἁμαρτίας.

4:1 Ἀρχὴ δὲ πάντων χαλεπῶν[7] φιλαργυρία.[8] εἰδότες οὖν ὅτι οὐδὲν εἰσηνέγκαμεν[9] εἰς τὸν κόσμον, ἀλλ' οὐδὲ ἐξενεγκεῖν[10] τι ἔχομεν, ὁπλισώμεθα[11] τοῖς ὅπλοις[12] τῆς δικαιοσύνης καὶ διδάξωμεν ἑαυτοὺς πρῶτον πορεύεσθαι ἐν τῇ ἐντολῇ τοῦ Κυρίου· **2** ἔπειτα[13] καὶ τὰς γυναῖκας ὑμῶν ἐν τῇ δοθείσῃ αὐταῖς πίστει καὶ ἀγάπῃ καὶ ἁγνείᾳ,[14] στεργούσας[15] τοὺς ἑαυτῶν ἄνδρας ἐν πάσῃ ἀληθείᾳ καὶ ἀγαπώσας πάντας ἐξ ἴσου[16] ἐν πάσῃ ἐγκρατείᾳ,[17] καὶ τὰ τέκνα παιδεύειν[18] τὴν παιδείαν[19] τοῦ φόβου τοῦ Θεοῦ· **3** τὰς χήρας[20] σωφρονούσας[21] περὶ τὴν τοῦ Κυρίου πίστιν, ἐντυγχανούσας[22] ἀδιαλείπτως[23] περὶ πάντων, μακρὰν[24] οὔσας πάσης διαβολῆς,[25] καταλαλιάς,[26] ψευδο-

---

[1] ἐγκύπτω pres act sub 2p, examine
[2] ἐπακολουθέω pres act ptcp f.s.gen., follow
[3] προάγω pres act ptcp f.s.gen., leads the way
[4] πλησίον, adv, neighbor
[5] ἐντός, prep (+ gen), inside, within, within the limits of
[6] μακράν, adv, far from
[7] χαλεπός, ή, όν, hard, difficult
[8] φιλαργυρία, ας, ἡ, love of money, avarice
[9] εἰσφέρω aor act ind 1p, bring in
[10] ἐκφέρω aor act inf, bring out
[11] ὁπλίζω aor mid sub 1p, equip, arm
[12] ὅπλον, ου, τό, weapon, tool

[13] ἔπειτα, adv, then
[14] ἁγνεία, ας, ἡ, purity
[15] στέργω pres act ptcp f.p.acc., love
[16] ἴσος, η, ον, equal
[17] ἐγκράτεια, ας, ἡ, self-control
[18] παιδεύω pres act inf, educate
[19] παιδεία, ας, ἡ, instruction
[20] χήρα, ας, ἡ, widow
[21] σωφρονέω pres act ptcp f.p.acc., sensible
[22] ἐντυγχάνω pres act ptcp f.p.acc., pray
[23] ἀδιαλείπτως, adv, unceasingly
[24] μακράν, adv, far away from
[25] διαβολή, ης, ἡ, slander
[26] καταλαλιά, ᾶς, ἡ, evil speech

μαρτυρίας,¹ φιλαργυρίας,² καὶ παντὸς κακοῦ, γινωσκούσας ὅτι
εἰσὶ θυσιαστήριον³ Θεοῦ καὶ ὅτι πάντα μωμοσκοπεῖται,⁴ καὶ
λέληθεν⁵ αὐτὸν οὐδὲν οὔτε λογισμῶν⁶ οὔτε ἐννοιῶν⁷ οὔτε τι τῶν
κρυπτῶν⁸ τῆς καρδίας.

5:1 Εἰδότες οὖν ὅτι Θεὸς οὐ μυκτηρίζεται,⁹ ὀφείλομεν ἀξίως¹⁰
τῆς ἐντολῆς αὐτοῦ καὶ δόξης περιπατεῖν. **2** ὁμοίως διάκονοι¹¹
ἄμεμπτοι¹² κατενώπιον¹³ αὐτοῦ τῆς δικαιοσύνης, ὡς Θεοῦ καὶ
Χριστοῦ διάκονοι,¹⁴ καὶ οὐκ ἀνθρώπων· μὴ διάβολοι, μὴ
δίλογοι,¹⁵ ἀφιλάργυροι,¹⁶ ἐγκρατεῖς¹⁷ περὶ πάντα,
εὔσπλαγχνοι,¹⁸ ἐπιμελεῖς,¹⁹ πορευόμενοι κατὰ τὴν ἀλήθειαν
τοῦ Κυρίου, ὃς ἐγένετο διάκονος²⁰ πάντων· ᾧ ἐὰν
εὐαρεστήσωμεν²¹ ἐν τῷ νῦν αἰῶνι, ἀποληψόμεθα²² καὶ τὸν
μέλλοντα, καθὼς ὑπέσχετο²³ ἡμῖν ἐγεῖραι ἡμᾶς ἐκ νεκρῶν καὶ
ὅτι, ἐὰν πολιτευσώμεθα²⁴ ἀξίως²⁵ αὐτοῦ, καὶ συμβασιλεύσομεν²⁶
αὐτῷ, εἴγε²⁷ πιστεύομεν. **3** Ὁμοίως καὶ νεώτεροι²⁸ ἄμεμπτοι²⁹ ἐν

---

¹ ψευδομαρτυρία, ας, ἡ, false witness
² φιλαργυρία, ας, ἡ, love of money, avarice
³ θυσιαστήριον, ου, ὁ, altar
⁴ μωμοσκοπέομαι pres mid/pass ind 3s, examine for blemishes
⁵ λανθάνω perf act ind 3s, be hidden, escape notice
⁶ λογισμός, οῦ, ὁ, thought
⁷ ἔννοια, ας, ἡ, knowledge
⁸ κρυπτός, ή, όν, hidden, secret
⁹ μυκτηρίζω pres mid/pass ind 3s, treat with contempt
¹⁰ ἀξίως, adv, worthily
¹¹ διάκονος, ου, ὁ, servant, assistant
¹² ἄμεμπτος, ον, blameless, faultless
¹³ κατενώπιον, prep (+ gen), before
¹⁴ διάκονος, ου, ὁ, servant, assistant
¹⁵ δίλογος, ον, insincere
¹⁶ αφιλάργυρος, ον, not greedy
¹⁷ ἐγκρατής, ές, self-controlled
¹⁸ εὔσπλαγχνος, ον, compassionate
¹⁹ ἐπιμελής, ές, careful, attentive
²⁰ διάκονος, ου, ὁ, servant, assistant
²¹ εὐαρεστέω aor act sub 1p, please
²² ἀπολαμβάνω fut mid ind 1p, receive, take
²³ ὑπισχνέομαι aor mid ind 3s, promise
²⁴ πολιτεύομαι aor mid sub 1p, have one's citizenship, home
²⁵ ἀξίως, adv, worthily
²⁶ συμβασιλεύω fut act ind 1p, reign jointly, rule with someone
²⁷ εἴγε, conj, if indeed
²⁸ νέος, νέα, young
²⁹ ἄμεμπτος, ον, blameless, without reproach

πᾶσιν· πρὸ παντὸς προνοοῦντες¹ ἀγνείας² καὶ χαλιν-
αγωγοῦντες³ ἑαυτοὺς ἀπὸ παντὸς κακοῦ. καλὸν γὰρ τὸ
ἀνακόπτεσθαι⁴ ἀπὸ τῶν ἐπιθυμιῶν ἐν τῷ κόσμῳ, ὅτι πᾶσα
ἐπιθυμία κατὰ τοῦ πνεύματος στρατεύεται,⁵ καὶ οὔτε πόρνοι⁶
οὔτε μαλακοὶ⁷ οὔτε ἀρσενοκοῖται⁸ βασιλείαν Θεοῦ
κληρονομήσουσιν,⁹ οὔτε οἱ ποιοῦντες τὰ ἄτοπα.¹⁰ διὸ δέον
ἀπέχεσθαι¹¹ ἀπὸ πάντων τούτων, ὑποτασσομένους τοῖς
πρεσβυτέροις καὶ διακόνοις¹² ὡς Θεῷ καὶ Χριστῷ. τὰς
παρθένους¹³ ἐν ἀμώμῳ¹⁴ καὶ ἁγνῇ¹⁵ συνειδήσει περιπατεῖν.

6:1 Καὶ οἱ πρεσβύτεροι δὲ εὔσπλαγχνοι,¹⁶ εἰς πάντας
ἐλεήμονες,¹⁷ ἐπιστρέφοντες τὰ ἀποπεπλανημένα,¹⁸ ἐπι-
σκεπτόμενοι¹⁹ πάντας ἀσθενεῖς,²⁰ μὴ ἀμελοῦντες²¹ χήρας ἢ
ὀρφανοῦ²² ἢ πένητος,²³ ἀλλὰ προνοοῦντες²⁴ ἀεὶ²⁵ τοῦ καλοῦ
ἐνώπιον Θεοῦ καὶ ἀνθρώπων, ἀπεχόμενοι²⁶ πάσης ὀργῆς,
προσωποληψίας,²⁷ κρίσεως ἀδίκου,²⁸ μακρὰν²⁹ ὄντες πάσης

---

¹ προνοέω pres act ptcp m.p.nom.,
  forsee
² ἀγνεία, ας, ἡ, purity
³ χαλιναγωγέω pres act ptcp
  m.p.nom., bridle
⁴ ἀνακόπτω pres mid/pass inf,
  hinder, restrain
⁵ στρατεύω pres mid/pass ind 3s,
  fight
⁶ πόρνος, ου, ὁ, fornicator
⁷ μαλακός, ή, όν, soft
⁸ ἀρσενοκοίτης, ου, ὁ, homosexual
⁹ κληρονομέω fut act ind 3p, inherit
¹⁰ ἄτοπος, ον, improper
¹¹ ἀπέχω pres mid/pass inf, receive
  in full
¹² διάκονος, ου, ὁ, servant, assistant
¹³ παρθένος, ου, ἡ, virgin
¹⁴ ἄμωμος, ον, blameless,
  unblemished
¹⁵ ἁγνός, ή, όν, pure, holy

¹⁶ εὔσπλαγχνος, ον, compassionate
¹⁷ ἐλεήμων, ον, merciful,
  compassionate
¹⁸ ἀποπλανάω perf mid/pass ptcp
  n.p.acc., go astray
¹⁹ ἐπισκέπτομαι pres mid/pass
  ptcp m.p.nom., visit
²⁰ ἀσθενής, ές, sick, ill
²¹ ἀμελέω pres act ptcp m.p.nom.,
  neglect, be unconcerned
²² ὀρφανός, ου, ὁ, orphan
²³ πένης, ητος, ὁ, poor, needy
²⁴ προνοέω pres act ptcp m.p.nom.,
  have regard for
²⁵ ἀεί, adv, always
²⁶ ἀπέχω pres mid/pass ptcp
  m.p.nom., keep away, refrain from
²⁷ προσωποληψία, ας, ἡ, partiality
²⁸ ἄδικος, ον, unjust, crooked
²⁹ μακράν, adv, far (away)

φιλαργυρίας,[1] μὴ ταχέως[2] πιστεύοντες κατά τινος, μὴ ἀπότομοι[3] ἐν κρίσει, εἰδότες ὅτι πάντες ὀφειλέται[4] ἐσμὲν ἁμαρτίας. **2** εἰ οὖν δεόμεθα[5] τοῦ Κυρίου ἵνα ἡμῖν ἀφῇ, ὀφείλομεν καὶ ἡμεῖς ἀφιέναι· ἀπέναντι[6] γὰρ τῶν τοῦ Κυρίου καὶ Θεοῦ ἐσμὲν ὀφθαλμῶν, καὶ πάντας δεῖ παραστῆναι τῷ βήματι[7] τοῦ Χριστοῦ, καὶ ἕκαστον ὑπὲρ ἑαυτοῦ λόγον δοῦναι. **3** οὕτως οὖν δουλεύσωμεν[8] αὐτῷ μετὰ φόβου καὶ πάσης εὐλαβείας,[9] καθὼς αὐτὸς ἐνετείλατο[10] καὶ οἱ εὐαγγελισάμενοι ἡμᾶς ἀπόστολοι καὶ οἱ προφῆται οἱ προκηρύξαντες[11] τὴν ἔλευσιν[12] τοῦ Κυρίου ἡμῶν, ζηλωταὶ[13] περὶ τὸ καλόν, ἀπεχόμενοι[14] τῶν σκανδάλων[15] καὶ τῶν ψευδαδέλφων[16] καὶ τῶν ἐν ὑποκρίσει[17] φερόντων τὸ ὄνομα τοῦ Κυρίου, οἵτινες ἀποπλανῶσι[18] κενοὺς[19] ἀνθρώπους

7:1 Πᾶς γὰρ ὃς ἂν μὴ ὁμολογῇ[20] Ἰησοῦν Χριστὸν ἐν σαρκὶ ἐληλυθέναι ἀντίχριστό[21] ἐστιν· καὶ ὃς ἂν μὴ ὁμολογῇ[22] τὸ μαρτύριον τοῦ σταυροῦ[23] ἐκ τοῦ διαβόλου ἐστίν· καὶ ὃς ἂν μεθοδεύῃ[24] τὰ λόγια[25] τοῦ Κυρίου πρὸς τὰς ἰδίας ἐπιθυμίας καὶ λέγῃ μήτε ἀνάστασιν μήτε κρίσιν, οὗτος πρωτότοκός[26] ἐστι τοῦ

---

[1] φιλαργυρία, ας, ἡ, love of money, miserliness
[2] ταχέως, adv, quickly
[3] ἀπότομος, ον, relentless
[4] ὀφειλέτης, ου, ὁ, debtor
[5] δέομαι pres mid/pass ind 1p, ask, request
[6] ἀπέναντι, prep (+ gen), opposite
[7] βῆμα, ατος, τό, judgment seat
[8] δουλεύω aor act sub 1p, serve
[9] εὐλάβεια, ας, ἡ, awe, fear of God
[10] ἐντέλλω aor mid ind 3s, command, give orders
[11] προκηρύσσω aor act ptcp m.p.nom., proclaim publicly
[12] ἔλευσις, εως, ἡ, arrival
[13] ζηλωτής, οῦ, ὁ, adherent, loyalist

[14] ἀπέχω pres mid/pass ptcp m.p.nom., keep away, refrain from
[15] σκάνδαλον, ου, τό, temptation to sin
[16] ψευδάδελφος, ου, ὁ, false brother
[17] ὑπόκρισις, εως, ἡ, insincerely
[18] ἀποπλανάω pres act ind 3p, mislead
[19] κενός, ή, όν, empty, vain
[20] ὁμολογέω pres act sub 3s, confess
[21] ἀντίχριστος, ου, ὁ, antichrist
[22] ὁμολογέω pres act sub 3s, confess
[23] σταυρός, ου, ὁ, cross
[24] μεθοδεύω pres act subj 3s, pervert
[25] λόγιον, ου, τό, saying
[26] πρωτότοκος, ον, firstborn

Σατανᾶ. **2** διὸ ἀπολιπόντες[1] τὴν ματαιότητα τῶν πολλῶν καὶ τὰς ψευδοδιδασκαλίας,[2] ἐπὶ τὸν ἐξ ἀρχῆς ἡμῖν παραδοθέντα λόγον ἐπιστρέψωμεν, νήφοντες[3] πρὸς τὰς εὐχὰς[4] καὶ προσκαρτεροῦντες[5] νηστείαις,[6] δεήσεσιν[7] αἰτούμενοι τὸν παντεπόπτην[8] Θεὸν μὴ εἰσενεγκεῖν[9] ἡμᾶς εἰς πειρασμόν,[10] καθὼς εἶπεν ὁ Κύριος· τὸ μὲν πνεῦμα πρόθυμον,[11] ἡ δὲ σὰρξ ἀσθενής.[12]

8:1 Ἀδιαλείπτως[13] οὖν προσκαρτερῶμεν[14] τῇ ἐλπίδι ἡμῶν καὶ τῷ ἀρραβῶνι[15] τῆς δικαιοσύνης ἡμῶν, ὅς ἐστι Χριστὸς Ἰησοῦς, ὃς ἀνήνεγκεν[16] ἡμῶν τὰς ἁμαρτίας τῷ ἰδίῳ σώματι ἐπὶ τὸ ξύλον,[17] ὃς ἁμαρτίαν οὐκ ἐποίησεν, οὐδὲ εὑρέθη δόλος[18] ἐν τῷ στόματι αὐτοῦ· ἀλλὰ δι᾽ ἡμᾶς, ἵνα ζήσωμεν ἐν αὐτῷ, πάντα ὑπέμεινεν.[19] **2** μιμηταὶ[20] οὖν γενώμεθα τῆς ὑπομονῆς αὐτοῦ, καὶ ἐὰν πάσχομεν διὰ τὸ ὄνομα αὐτοῦ, δοξάζωμεν αὐτόν. τοῦτον γὰρ ἡμῖν τὸν ὑπογραμμὸν[21] ἔθηκε δι᾽ ἑαυτοῦ, καὶ ἡμεῖς τοῦτο ἐπιστεύσαμεν.

9:1 Παρακαλῶ οὖν πάντας ὑμᾶς πειθαρχεῖν[22] τῷ λόγῳ τῆς δικαιοσύνης καὶ ἀσκεῖν[23] πᾶσαν ὑπομονήν, ἣν καὶ εἴδατε κατ᾽

---

[1] ἀπολείπω aor act ptcp m.p.nom., put aside, leave behind
[2] ψευδοδιδασκαλία, ας, ἡ, false teaching
[3] νήφω pres act ptcp m.p.nom., self-controlled
[4] εὐχή, ῆς, ἡ, prayer
[5] προσκαρτερέω pres act ptcp m.p.nom., continue in
[6] νηστεία, ας, ἡ, fast
[7] δέησις, εως, ἡ, prayer
[8] παντεπόπτης, ου, ὁ, one who is all-seeing
[9] εἰσφέρω aor act inf, bring in
[10] πειρασμός, ου, ὁ, temptation
[11] πρόθυμος, ον, willing
[12] ἀσθενής, ές, weak
[13] ἀδιαλείπτως, adv, constantly, unceasingly
[14] προσκαρτερέω pres act sub 1p, hold fast to, persevere in
[15] ἀρραβών, ῶνος, ὁ, pledge
[16] ἀναφέρω aor act ind 3s, take up
[17] ξύλον, ου, τό, tree
[18] δόλος, ου, ὁ, deceit, cunning
[19] ὑπομένω aor act ind 3s, endure
[20] μιμητής, οῦ, ὁ, imitator
[21] ὑπογραμμός, οῦ, ὁ, example
[22] πειθαρχέω pres act inf, obey
[23] ἀσκέω pres act inf, practice

ὀφθαλμοὺς οὐ μόνον ἐν τοῖς μακαρίοις Ἰγνατίῳ[1] καὶ Ζωσίμῳ[2] καὶ Ῥούφῳ[3] ἀλλὰ καὶ ἐν ἄλλοις τοῖς ἐξ ὑμῶν καὶ ἐν αὐτῷ Παύλῳ καὶ τοῖς λοιποῖς ἀποστόλοις· **2** πεπεισμένους ὅτι οὗτοι πάντες οὐκ εἰς κενὸν[4] ἔδραμον[5] ἀλλ᾽ ἐν πίστει καὶ δικαιοσύνῃ, καὶ ὅτι εἰς τὸν ὀφειλόμενον αὐτοῖς τόπον εἰσὶ παρὰ τῷ Κυρίῳ, ᾧ καὶ συνέπαθον.[6] οὐ γὰρ τὸν νῦν ἠγάπησαν αἰῶνα, ἀλλὰ τὸν ὑπὲρ ἡμῶν ἀποθανόντα καὶ δι᾽ ἡμᾶς ὑπὸ τοῦ Θεοῦ ἀναστάντα...

... **13** Ἐγράψατέ μοι καὶ ὑμεῖς καὶ Ἰγνάτιος[7] ἵνα, ἐάν τις ἀπέρχηται εἰς Συρίαν,[8] καὶ τὰ παρ᾽ ὑμῶν ἀποκομίσῃ[9] γράμματα· ὅπερ[10] ποιήσω, ἐὰν λάβω καιρὸν εὔθετον,[11] εἴτε ἐγὼ εἴτε ὃν πέμψω πρεσβεύσοντα[12] καὶ περὶ ὑμῶν. **2** τὰς ἐπιστολὰς Ἰγνατίου[13] τὰς πεμφθείσας ἡμῖν ὑπ᾽ αὐτοῦ, καὶ ἄλλας ὅσας εἴχομεν παρ᾽ ἡμῖν, ἐπέμψαμεν ὑμῖν, καθὼς ἐνετείλασθε·[14] αἵτινες ὑποτεταγμέναι εἰσὶν τῇ ἐπιστολῇ ταύτῃ· ἐξ ὧν μεγάλα ὠφεληθῆναι[15] δυνήσεσθε. περιέχουσι γὰρ πίστιν καὶ ὑπομονὴν καὶ πᾶσαν οἰκοδομὴν[16] τὴν εἰς τὸν Κύριον ἡμῶν ἀνήκουσαν.[17]

---

[1] Ἰγνάτιος, ου, ὁ, Ignatius
[2] Ζώσιμος, ου, ὁ, Zosimus
[3] Ῥοῦφος, ου, ὁ, Rufus
[4] κενός, ή, όν, vain
[5] τρέχω aor act ind 3p, run
[6] συμπάσχω aor act ind 3p, suffer with
[7] Ἰγνάτιος, ου, ὁ, Ignatius
[8] Συρία, ας, ἡ, Syria
[9] ἀποκομίζω aor act sub 3s, take along
[10] ὅσπερ, ἥπερ, ὅπερ, this

[11] εὔθετος, ον, fit, suitable
[12] πρεσβεύω fut act ptcp m.s.acc., be an ambassador
[13] Ἰγνάτιος, ου, ὁ, Ignatius
[14] ἐντέλλω aor mid ind 2p, command, order
[15] περιέχω pres act ind 3p, contain
[16] οἰκοδομή, ῆς, ἡ, building, construction
[17] ἀνήκω pres act ptcp f.s.acc., belong, pertain

ΜΑΡΤΥΡΙΟΝ ΤΟΥ ΑΓΙΟΥ ΠΟΛΥΚΑΡΠΟΥ ΕΠΙΣΚΟΠΟΥ ΣΜΥΡΝΗΣ

NOTES BY SHAWN J. WILHITE

Ἡ ἐκκλησία τοῦ θεοῦ ἡ παροικοῦσα[1] Σμύρναν[2] τῇ ἐκκλησίᾳ τοῦ θεοῦ τῇ παροικούσῃ[3] ἐν Φιλομηλίῳ[4] καὶ πάσαις ταῖς κατὰ πάντα τόπον τῆς ἁγίας καὶ καθολικῆς[5] ἐκκλησίας παροικίαις·[6] ἔλεος[7] εἰρήνη καὶ ἀγάπη θεοῦ πατρὸς καὶ κυρίου ἡμῶν Ἰησοῦ Χριστοῦ πληθυνθείη.[8]

1:1 Ἐγράψαμεν ὑμῖν, ἀδελφοί, τὰ κατὰ τοὺς μαρτυρήσαντας καὶ τὸν μακάριον Πολύκαρπον,[9] ὅστις ὥσπερ ἐπισφραγίσας[10] διὰ τῆς μαρτυρίας αὐτοῦ κατέπαυσεν[11] τὸν διωγμόν.[12] σχεδὸν[13] γὰρ πάντα τὰ προάγοντα[14] ἐγένετο, ἵνα ἡμῖν ὁ κύριος ἄνωθεν[15] ἐπιδείξῃ[16] τὸ κατὰ τὸ εὐαγγέλιον μαρτύριον.[17] **2** περιέμενεν[18] γὰρ, ἵνα παραδοθῇ, ὡς καὶ ὁ κύριος, ἵνα μιμηταὶ[19] καὶ ἡμεῖς

---

[1] παροικέω pres act ptcp f.s.nom., inhabit a place as a foreigner, be a stranger
[2] Σμύρνα, ης, ἡ, Smyrna
[3] παροικέω pres act ptcp f.s.dat., inhabit a place as a foreigner, be a stranger
[4] Φιλομήλιον, ου, τό, Philomelium
[5] καθολικός, ή, όν, general, universal
[6] παροικία, ας, ἡ, sojourn
[7] ἔλεος, ους, τό, mercy
[8] πληθύνω aor pass opt 3s, increase, multiply
[9] Πολύκαρπος, ου, ὁ, Polycarp
[10] ἐπισφραγίζω aor act ptcp m.s.nom., seal, put a seal on something
[11] καταπαύω aor act ind 3s, cease, rest, bring to an end
[12] διωγμός, οῦ, ὁ, persecution
[13] σχεδόν, adv, nearly, almost
[14] προάγω pres act ptcp n.p.nom., go before, precede
[15] ἄνωθεν, adv, from above
[16] ἐπιδείκνυμι aor act sub 3s, point out, demonstrate
[17] μαρτύριον, ου, τό, martyrdom
[18] περιμένω imp act ind 3s, wait for
[19] μιμητής, οῦ, ὁ, imitator

αὐτοῦ γενώμεθα, μὴ μόνον σκοποῦντες[1] τὸ καθ᾽ ἑαυτούς, ἀλλὰ καὶ τὸ κατὰ τοὺς πέλας.[2] ἀγάπης γὰρ ἀληθοῦς[3] καὶ βεβαίας[4] ἐστίν, μὴ μόνον ἑαυτὸν θέλειν σῴζεσθαι, ἀλλὰ καὶ πάντας τοὺς ἀδελφούς.

2:1 Μακάρια μὲν οὖν καὶ γενναῖα[5] τὰ μαρτύρια[6] πάντα τὰ κατὰ τὸ θέλημα τοῦ θεοῦ γεγονότα. δεῖ γὰρ εὐλαβεστέρους[7] ἡμᾶς ὑπάρχοντας τῷ θεῷ τὴν κατὰ πάντων ἐξουσίαν ἀνατιθέναι.[8] **2** τὸ γὰρ γενναῖον[9] αὐτῶν καὶ ὑπομονητικὸν[10] καὶ φιλοδέσποτον[11] τίς οὐκ ἂν θαυμάσειεν; οἱ μάστιξιν[12] μὲν καταξανθέντες,[13] ὥστε μέχρι[14] τῶν ἔσω[15] φλεβῶν[16] καὶ ἀρτηριῶν[17] τὴν τῆς σαρκὸς οἰκονομίαν[18] θεωρεῖσθαι, ὑπέμειναν,[19] ὡς καὶ τοὺς περιεστῶτας[20] ἐλεεῖν[21] καὶ ὀδύρεσθαι.[22] τοὺς δὲ καὶ εἰς τοσοῦτον[23] γενναιότητος[24] ἐλθεῖν, ὥστε μήτε γρύξαι[25] μήτε στενάξαι[26] τινὰ αὐτῶν, ἐπιδεικνυμένους,[27] ἅπασιν ἡμῖν, ὅτι

---

[1] σκοπέω pres act ptcp m.p.nom., pay careful attention to, look out for
[2] πέλας, adv, near
[3] ἀληθής, ές, true
[4] βέβαιος, α, ον, reliable, unshifting, steadfast
[5] γενναῖος, α, ον, noble
[6] μαρτύριον, ου, τό, martyrdom
[7] εὐλαβής, ές, devout, god-fearing
[8] ἀνατίθημι pres act inf, ascribe, attribute
[9] γενναῖος, α, ον, noble
[10] ὑπομονητικός, ή, όν, patient, showing endurance
[11] φιλοδέσποτος, ον, loving one's master
[12] μάστιξ, ιγος, ἡ, whip, lash
[13] καταξαίνω aor pass ptcp m.p.nom., tear to shreds
[14] μέχρι, adv, until
[15] ἔσω, adv, inside
[16] φλέψ, φλεβός, ἡ, vein
[17] ἀρτηρία, ας, ἡ, artery
[18] οἰκονομία, ας, ἡ, structure, arrangement
[19] ὑπομένω aor act ind 3p, endure, remain
[20] περιίστημι perf act ptcp m.p.acc., stand around
[21] ἐλεέω pres act inf, have mercy, pity
[22] ὀδύρομαι pres mid/pass inf, mourn, lament
[23] τοσοῦτος, αύτη, οῦτον, so great, so many
[24] γενναιότης, ητος, ἡ, nobility, bravery
[25] γρύζω aor act inf, mutter, complain
[26] στενάζω aor act inf, sigh, groan
[27] ἐπιδείκνυμι pres mid/pass ptcp m.p.acc. point out, demonstrate

ἐκείνῃ τῇ ὥρᾳ βασανιζόμενοι[1] τῆς σαρκὸς ἀπεδήμουν[2] οἱ γενναιότατοι[3] μάρτυρες τοῦ Χριστοῦ, μᾶλλον δὲ, ὅτι παρεστὼς ὁ κύριος ὡμίλει[4] αὐτοῖς. **3** καὶ προσέχοντες[5] τῇ τοῦ Χριστοῦ χάριτι τῶν κοσμικῶν[6] κατεφρόνουν[7] βασάνων,[8] διὰ μιᾶς ὥρας τὴν αἰώνιον ζωὴν ἐξαγοραζόμενοι.[9] καὶ τὸ πῦρ ἦν αὐτοῖς ψυχρὸν[10] τὸ τῶν ἀπηνῶν[11] βασανιστῶν.[12] πρὸ ὀφθαλμῶν γὰρ εἶχον φυγεῖν[13] τὸ αἰώνιον καὶ μηδέποτε[14] σβεννύμενον,[15] καὶ τοῖς τῆς καρδίας ὀφθαλμοῖς ἀνέβλεπον[16] τὰ τηρούμενα τοῖς ὑπομείνασιν[17] ἀγαθά, ἃ οὔτε οὖς ἤκουσεν οὔτε ὀφθαλμὸς εἶδεν οὔτε ἐπὶ καρδίαν ἀνθρώπου ἀνέβη, ἐκείνοις δὲ ὑπεδείκνυτο[18] ὑπὸ τοῦ κυρίου, οἵπερ[19] μηκέτι[20] ἄνθρωποι, ἀλλ' ἤδη ἄγγελοι ἦσαν. **4** ὁμοίως[21] δὲ καὶ οἱ εἰς τὰ θηρία κατακριθέντες,[22] ὑπέμειναν[23] δεινὰς[24] κολάσεις,[25] κήρυκας[26] ὑποστρωννύμενοι[27]

---

[1] βασανίζω pres mid/pass ptcp m.p.nom., torture

[2] ἀποδημέω imp act ind 3p, absent

[3] γενναιότης, ητος, ἡ, nobility, bravery

[4] ὁμιλέω imp act ind 3s, converse, address

[5] προσέχω pres act ptcp m.p.nom., pay attention to, devote oneself to

[6] κοσμικός, ή, όν, wordily

[7] καταφρονέω imp act ind 3p, look down upon, despise

[8] βάσανος, ου, ἡ, torture

[9] ἐξαγοράζω pres mid/pass ptcp m.p.nom., deliver, liberate

[10] ψυχρός, ά, όν, cold (lit.), without enthusiasm

[11] ἀπηνής, ής, ές, rough, wild

[12] βασανιστής, οῦ, ὁ, oppressive jailer, torturer

[13] φεύγω aor act inf, flee, escape

[14] μηδέποτε, adv, never

[15] σβέννυμι pres mid/pass ptcp n.s.acc., quench, extinguish

[16] ἀναβλέπω imp act ind 3p, look upon, regain sight

[17] ὑπομένω aor act ptcp m.p.dat., endure, remain

[18] ὑποδείκνυμι imp act ind 3s, point out, show

[19] ὅς, ἥ, ὅ, who, which, what

[20] μηκέτι, adv, no longer

[21] ὁμοίως, adv, likewise

[22] κατακρίνω aor pass ptcp m.p.nom., pronounce a sentence, condemn

[23] ὑπομένω aor act ind 3p, endure, remain

[24] δεινός, ή, όν, fearful, terrible

[25] κόλασις, εως, ἡ, punishment

[26] κῆρυξ, υκος, ὁ, trumpet shell

[27] ὑποστρωννύω/ὑποστρώννυμι pres mid/pass ptcp m.p.nom., spread out underneath

καὶ ἄλλαις ποικίλων[1] βασάνων[2] ἰδέαις[3] κολαζόμενοι,[4] ἵνα, εἰ δυνηθείη, διὰ τῆς ἐπιμόνου[5] κολάσεως[6] εἰς ἄρνησιν[7] αὐτοὺς τρέψῃ.[8] πολλὰ γὰρ ἐμηχανᾶτο[9] κατ' αὐτῶν ὁ διάβολος.

3:1 Ἀλλὰ χάρις τῷ θεῷ κατὰ πάντων γὰρ οὐκ ἴσχυσεν.[10] ὁ γὰρ γενναιότατος[11] Γερμανικὸς[12] ἐπερρώννυεν[13] αὐτῶν τὴν δειλίαν[14] διὰ τῆς ἐν αὐτῷ ὑπομονῆς· ὃς καὶ ἐπισήμως[15] ἐθηριομάχησεν.[16] βουλομένου γὰρ τοῦ ἀνθυπάτου[17] πείθειν αὐτὸν καὶ λέγοντος, τὴν ἡλικίαν[18] αὐτοῦ κατοικτεῖραι,[19] ἑαυτῷ ἐπεσπάσατο[20] τὸ θηρίον προσβιασάμενος,[21] τάχιον[22] τοῦ ἀδίκου[23] καὶ ἀνόμου[24] βίου[25] αὐτῶν ἀπαλλαγῆναι[26] βουλόμενος. **2** ἐκ τούτου οὖν πᾶν τὸ πλῆθος, θαυμάσαν τὴν γενναιότητα[27] τοῦ θεοφιλοῦς[28] καὶ θεοσεβοῦς γένους[29] τῶν Χριστιανῶν,[30] ἐπεβόησεν.[31] Αἶρε τοὺς ἀθέους·[32] ζητείσθω Πολύκαρπος.[33]

---

[1] ποικίλος, η, ον, diverse, variegated
[2] βάσανος, ου, ἡ, torture
[3] ἰδέα, ας, ἡ, appearance
[4] κολάζω pres mid/pass ptcp m.p.nom., penalize, punish
[5] ἐπίμονος, ον, continuous
[6] κόλασις, εως, ἡ, punishment
[7] ἄρνησις, εως, ἡ, rejection, denial
[8] τρέπω aor act sub 3s, turn
[9] μηχανάομαι imp mid/pass ind 3s, devise, contrive
[10] ἰσχύω aor act ind 3s, be able, be strong
[11] γενναῖος, α, ον, noble
[12] Γερμανικός, οῦ, ὁ, Germanicus
[13] ἐπιρρώννυμι imp act ind 3s, strengthen, encourage
[14] δειλία, ας, ἡ, cowardice
[15] ἐπισήμως, adv, in an outstanding manner
[16] θηριομαχέω aor act ind 3s, fight with animals
[17] ἀνθύπατος, ου, ὁ, procounsul
[18] ἡλικία, ας, ἡ, age, time of life
[19] κατοικτίρω pres act inf, have mercy
[20] ἐπισπάω aor mid ind 3s, draw to oneself
[21] προσβιάζομαι aor mid ptcp m.s.nom., compel, use force
[22] ταχέως, adv, quickly
[23] ἄδικος, ον, unjust
[24] ἄνομος, ον, lawless
[25] βίος, ου, ὁ, life
[26] ἀπαλλάσσω aor pass inf, free, release
[27] γενναιότης, ητος, ἡ, nobility, bravery
[28] θεοφιλής, ές, loving God
[29] γένος, ους, τό, nation, race
[30] Χριστιανός, οῦ, ὁ, Christian
[31] ἐπιβοάω aor act ind 3s, cry out loudly
[32] ἄθεος, ον, without God, athiest
[33] Πολύκαρπος, ου, ὁ, Polycarp

17

4:1 Εἷς δὲ, ὀνόματι Κόϊντος,[1] Φρὺξ[2] προσφάτως[3] ἐληλυθὼς ἀπὸ τῆς Φρυγίας,[4] ἰδὼν τὰ θηρία ἐδειλίασεν.[5] οὗτος δὲ ἦν ὁ παραβιασάμενος[6] ἑαυτόν τε καὶ τινας προσελθεῖν ἑκόντας.[7] τοῦτον ὁ ἀνθύπατος[8] πολλὰ ἐκλιπαρήσας[9] ἔπεισεν ὀμόσαι[10] καὶ ἐπιθῦσαι.[11] διὰ τοῦτο οὖν, ἀδελφοί, οὐκ ἐπαινοῦμεν[12] τοὺς προδιδόντας[13] ἑαυτούς, ἐπειδὴ[14] οὐχ οὕτως διδάσκει τὸ εὐαγγέλιον.

5:1 Ὁ δὲ θαυμασιώτατος[15] Πολύκαρπος[16] τὸ μὲν πρῶτον ἀκούσας οὐκ ἐταράχθη,[17] ἀλλ' ἐβούλετο κατὰ πόλιν μένειν· οἱ δὲ πλείους ἔπειθον αὐτὸν ὑπεξελθεῖν.[18] καὶ ὑπεξῆλθεν[19] εἰς ἀγρίδιον[20] οὐ μακρὰν[21] ἀπέχον[22] ἀπὸ τῆς πόλεως καὶ διέτριβεν[23] μετ' ὀλίγων, νύκτα καὶ ἡμέραν οὐδὲν ἕτερον ποιῶν ἢ προσ-ευχόμενος περὶ πάντων καὶ τῶν κατὰ τὴν οἰκουμένην[24] ἐκ-κλησίων, ὅπερ[25] ἦν σύνηθες[26] αὐτῷ. **2** καὶ προσευχόμενος ἐν

---

[1] Κόϊντος, ου, ὁ, Quintus
[2] Φρύξ, γός, ὁ, Phrygian
[3] προσφάτως, adv, recently
[4] Φρυγία, ας, ἡ, Phrygia
[5] δειλιάω aor act ind 3s, be cowardly, be fearful
[6] παραβιάζομαι aor mid ptcp m.s.nom., urge strongly, prevail upon
[7] ἑκών, οῦσα, όν, willingly, gladly
[8] ἀνθύπατος, ου, ὁ, proconsul
[9] ἐκλιπαρέω aor act ptcp m.s.nom., beg, entreat
[10] ὀμνύω aor act inf, swear, take an oath
[11] ἐπιθύω aor act inf, offer a sacrifice
[12] ἐπαινέω pres act ind 1p, praise
[13] προδίδωμι pres act ptcp m.p.acc., hand over, betray
[14] ἐπειδή, conj, since, because

[15] θαυμάσιος, α, ον, wonderful, remarkable
[16] Πολύκαρπος, ου, ὁ, Polycarp
[17] ταράσσω aor pass ind 3s, inward turmoil, disturb
[18] ὑπεξέρχομαι aor act inf, go out quietly, go out secretly
[19] ὑπεξέρχομαι aor act ind 3s, go out quietly, go out secretly
[20] ἀγρίδιον, ου, τό, little farm, country house
[21] μακράν, adv, far away
[22] ἀπέχω pres act ptcp n.s.acc., distant
[23] διατρίβω imp act ind 3s, spend time
[24] οἰκουμένη, ης, ἡ, inhabited earth, the world
[25] ὅσπερ, ἥπερ, ὅπερ, who indeed
[26] συνήθης, ες, habitual, customary

ὀπτασία[1] γέγονεν πρὸ τριῶν ἡμερῶν τοῦ συλληφθῆναι[2] αὐτόν, καὶ εἶδεν τὸ προσκεφάλαιον[3] αὐτοῦ ὑπὸ πυρὸς κατακαιόμενον·[4] καὶ στραφεὶς[5] εἶπεν πρὸς τοὺς σὺν αὐτῷ Δεῖ με ζῶντα καῆναι.[6]

6:1 Καὶ ἐπιμενόντων[7] τῶν ζητούντων αὐτόν μετέβη·[8] εἰς ἕτερον ἀγρίδιον,[9] καὶ μὴ εὑρόντες συνελάβοντο[10] παιδάρια[11] δύο, ὧν τὸ ἕτερον βασανιζόμενον[12] ὡμολόγησεν.[13] **2** ἦν γὰρ καὶ ἀδύνατον[14] λαθεῖν[15] αὐτόν, ἐπεὶ[16] καὶ οἱ προδιδόντες[17] αὐτὸν οἰκεῖοι[18] ὑπῆρχον, καὶ ὁ εἰρήναρχος,[19] ὁ κεκληρωμένος[20] τὸ αὐτὸ ὄνομα, Ἡρώδης ἐπιλεγόμενος,[21] ἔσπευδεν[22] εἰς τὸ στάδιον[23] αὐτὸν εἰσαγαγεῖν,[24] ἵνα ἐκεῖνος μὲν τὸν ἴδιον κλῆρον[25] ἀπαρτίσῃ[26]

---

[1] ὀπτασία, ας, ἡ, vision, trance

[2] συλλαμβάνω aor pass inf, seize, grasp, apprehend

[3] προσκεφάλαιον, ου, τό, pillow, cushion

[4] κατακαίω pres mid/pass ptcp n.s.acc., consume, burn up

[5] στρέφω aor pass ptcp m.s.nom., turn around

[6] καίω aor pass inf, burn, light

[7] ἐπιμένω pres act ptcp m.p.gen., continue, persevere

[8] μεταβαίνω aor act ind 3s, go/pass over

[9] ἀγρίδιον, ου, τό, little farm, country

[10] συλλαμβάνω aor mid ind 3p, seize, grasp, apprehend

[11] παιδάριον, ου, τό, young slave

[12] βασανίζω pres mid/pass ptcp n.s.acc., torture

[13] ὁμολογέω aor act ind 3s, confess, admit

[14] ἀδύνατος, ον, impossible

[15] λανθάνω aor act inf, be hidden, escape notice

[16] ἐπεί, conj, because, since

[17] προδίδωμι pres act ptcp m.p.nom., betray

[18] οἰκεῖος, (α), ον, members of a household

[19] εἰρήναρχος, ου, ὁ, chief of police, police captain

[20] κληρόω perf mid/pass ptcp m.s.nom., obtain by lot

[21] ἐπιλέγω pres mid/pass ptcp m.s.nom., call/name (in addition)

[22] σπεύδω imp act ind 3s, hurry, hasten

[23] στάδιον, ου, τό, stadium, arena

[24] εἰσάγω aor act inf, bring or lead into

[25] κλῆρος, ου, ὁ, lot, destiny

[26] ἀπαρτίζω aor act sub 3s, finish, complete

Χριστοῦ κοινωνὸς[1] γενόμενος, οἱ δὲ προδόντες[2] αὐτὸν τὴν αὐτοῦ τοῦ Ἰούδα[3] ὑπόσχοιεν[4] τιμωρίαν.[5]

7:1 Ἔχοντες οὖν τὸ παιδάριον,[6] τῇ παρασκευῇ[7] περὶ δείπνου[8] ὥραν ἐξῆλθον διωγμῖται[9] καὶ ἱππεῖς[10] μετὰ τῶν συνήθων[11] αὐτοῖς ὅπλων[12] ὡς ἐπὶ λῃστὴν[13] τρέχοντες.[14] καὶ ὀψὲ[15] τῆς ὥρας συνεπελθόντες[16] ἐκεῖνον μὲν εὗρον ἐν ὑπερῴῳ[17] κατακείμενον· κἀκεῖθεν[18] δὲ ἠδύνατο εἰς ἕτερον χωρίον[19] ἀπελθεῖν, ἀλλ᾽ οὐκ ἠβουλήθη εἰπών· Τὸ θέλημα τοῦ θεοῦ γενέσθω. **2** ἀκούσας οὖν παρόντας[20] αὐτούς, καταβὰς διελέχθη[21] αὐτοῖς, θαυμαζόντων τῶν παρόντων[22] τὴν ἡλικίαν[23] αὐτοῦ καὶ τὸ εὐσταθές,[24] καὶ εἰ τοσαύτη[25] σπουδὴ[26] ἦν τοῦ συλληφθῆναι[27] τοιοῦτον πρεσβύτην[28] ἄνδρα. εὐθέως οὖν αὐτοῖς ἐκέλευσεν[29] παρατεθῆναι[30] φαγεῖν

---

[1] κοινωνός, οῦ, ὁ, companion, sharer

[2] προδίδωμι aor act ptcp m.p.nom., betray

[3] Ἰούδας, α, ὁ, Judas

[4] ὑπέχω aor act opt 3p, undergo punishment

[5] τιμωρία, ας, ἡ, punishment

[6] παιδάριον, ου, τό, young slave

[7] παρασκευή, ῆς, ἡ, Friday (day of preparation)

[8] δεῖπνον, ου, τό, dinner

[9] διωγμίτης, ου, ὁ, detective, (mounted) security officer

[10] ἱππεύς, έως, ὁ, horse rider

[11] συνήθης, ες, usual, customary

[12] ὅπλον, ου, τό, weapon

[13] λῃστής, οῦ, ὁ, robber, bandit

[14] τρέχω pres act ptcp m.p.nom., run, advance

[15] ὀψέ, adv, late

[16] συνεπέρχομαι aor act ptcp m.p.nom., come together against, attack together

[17] ὑπερῷος, (α), ον, upstairs, in the upper story under the roof

[18] κἀκεῖθεν, adv, from there

[19] χωρίον, ου, τό, place, piece of land

[20] πάρειμι pres act ptcp m.p.acc., present

[21] διαλέγομαι aor pass ind 3s, converse, discuss

[22] πάρειμι pres act ptcp m.p.gen., present

[23] ἡλικία, ας, ἡ, age, time of life

[24] εὐσταθής, ές, composure, calm

[25] τοσοῦτος, αύτη, οῦτον, so great, to such extent

[26] σπουδή, ῆς, ἡ, eagerness, diligence, zeal

[27] συλλαμβάνω aor pass inf, sieze, apprehend

[28] πρεσβύτης, ου, ὁ, old man, aged man

[29] κελεύω aor act ind 3s, command, urge

[30] παρατίθημι aor pass inf, set before

καὶ πιεῖν ἐν ἐκείνῃ τῇ ὥρᾳ, ὅσον ἂν βούλωνται, ἐξητήσατο¹ δὲ αὐτούς, ἵνα δῶσιν αὐτῷ ὥραν πρὸς τὸ προσεύξασθαι ἀδεῶς.² **3** τῶν δὲ ἐπιτρεψάντων,³ σταθεὶς προσηύξατο πλήρης⁴ ὢν τῆς χάριτος τοῦ θεοῦ οὕτως ὥστε ἐπὶ δύο ὥρας μὴ δύνασθαι σιγῆσαι⁵ καὶ ἐκπλήττεσθαι⁶ τοὺς ἀκούοντας, πολλούς τε μετανοεῖν ἐπὶ τῷ ἐληλυθέναι ἐπὶ τοιοῦτον θεοπρεπῆ⁷ πρεσβύτην.⁸

8:1 Ἐπεὶ⁹ δέ ποτε¹⁰ κατέπαυσεν¹¹ τὴν προσευχήν, μνημονεύσας¹² ἁπάντων καὶ τῶν πώποτε¹³ συμβεβληκότων¹⁴ αὐτῷ, μικρῶν τε καὶ μεγάλων, ἐνδόξων¹⁵ τε καὶ ἀδόξων¹⁶ καὶ πάσης τῆς κατὰ τὴν οἰκουμένην¹⁷ καθολικῆς¹⁸ ἐκκλησίας, τῆς ὥρας ἐλθούσης τοῦ ἐξιέναι,¹⁹ ὄνῳ²⁰ καθίσαντες αὐτὸν ἤγαγον εἰς τὴν πόλιν, ὄντος σαββάτου μεγάλου. **2** καὶ ὑπήντα²¹ αὐτῷ ὁ εἰρήναρχος²² Ἡρώδης καὶ ὁ πατὴρ αὐτοῦ Νικήτης,²³ οἳ καὶ

¹ ἐξαιτέω aor mid ind 3s, ask
² ἀδεῶς, adv, without disturbance
³ ἐπιτρέπω aor act ptcp m.p.gen., allow, permit
⁴ πλήρης, ες, full, filled
⁵ σιγάω aor act inf, stop speaking, become silent
⁶ ἐκπλήσσω pres mid/pass inf, amaze, astound
⁷ θεοπρεπής, ές, worthy of God, godly
⁸ πρεσβύτης, ου, ὁ, old man, aged man
⁹ ἐπεί, conj, because, since
¹⁰ ποτέ, adv, at some time
¹¹ καταπαύω aor act ind 3s, cease, bring to an end
¹² μνημονεύω aor act ptcp m.s.nom., remember, think of
¹³ πώποτε, adv, ever, at any time
¹⁴ συμβάλλω perf act ptcp m.p.gen., meet
¹⁵ ἔνδοξος, ον, honored, distinguished
¹⁶ ἄδοξος, ον, without reputation, obscure
¹⁷ οἰκουμένη, ης, ἡ, inhabited earth, world
¹⁸ καθολικός, ή, όν, general, universal
¹⁹ ἔξειμι pres act inf, depart, go away
²⁰ ὄνος, ου, ὁ, (domesticated) ass, donkey
²¹ ὑπαντάω imp act ind 3s, meet
²² εἰρήναρχος, ου, ὁ, chief of police, police captain
²³ Νικήτης, ου, Nicetes

μεταθέντες[1] αὐτὸν ἐπὶ τὴν καροῦχαν[2] ἔπειθον παρα-
καθεζόμενοι[3] καὶ λέγοντες· Τί γὰρ κακόν ἐστιν εἰπεῖν· Κύριος
καῖσαρ,[4] καὶ ἐπιθῦσαι[5] καὶ τὰ τούτοις ἀκόλουθα[6] καὶ
διασώζεσθαι;[7] ὁ δὲ τὰ μὲν πρῶτα οὐκ ἀπεκρίνατο αὐτοῖς,
ἐπιμενόντων[8] δὲ αὐτῶν ἔφη· Οὐ μέλλω ποιεῖν, ὃ συμβουλεύετέ[9]
μοι. 3 οἱ δέ ἀποτυχόντες[10] τοῦ πεῖσαι αὐτόν δεινὰ[11] ῥήματα
ἔλεγον αὐτῷ καὶ μετὰ σπουδῆς[12] καθῄρουν[13] αὐτόν, ὡς
κατιόντα[14] ἀπὸ τῆς καρούχας[15] ἀποσῦραι[16] τὸ ἀντικνήμιον.[17] καὶ
μὴ ἐπιστραφείς, ὡς οὐδὲν πεπονθώς προθύμως[18] μετὰ σπουδῆς[19]
ἐπορεύετο, ἀγόμενος εἰς τὸ στάδιον,[20] θορύβου[21] τηλικούτου[22]
ὄντος ἐν τῷ σταδίῳ,[23] ὡς μηδὲ ἀκουσθῆναί τινα δύνασθαι.

9:1 Τῷ δὲ Πολυκάρπῳ[24] εἰσιόντι[25] εἰς τὸ στάδιον[26] φωνὴ ἐξ
οὐρανοῦ ἐγένετο· Ἴσχυε,[27] Πολύκαρπε,[28] καὶ ἀνδρίζου.[29] καὶ τὸν

---

[1] μετατίθημι aor act ptcp
  m.p.nom., put in another place,
  transfer
[2] καροῦχα, ας, ἡ, carriage
[3] παρακαθέζομαι pres mid/pass
  ptcp m.p.nom., set aside
[4] καῖσαρ, αρος, ὁ, Caesar
[5] ἐπιθύω aor act inf, offer a sacrifice
[6] ἀκόλουθος, ον, following
  (sequence)
[7] διασώζω pres mid/pass inf, bring
  safely through, rescuer
[8] ἐπιμένω pres act ptcp m.p.gen.,
  stay, remain, persist
[9] συμβουλεύω pres act ind 2p,
  advise
[10] ἀποτυγχάνω aor act ptcp
  m.p.nom., fail
[11] δεινός, ή, όν, fearful, terrible
[12] σπουδή, ῆς, ἡ, haste, speed
[13] καθαιρέω imp act ind 3p, take
  down, bring down, lower

[14] κάτειμι pres act ptcp m.s.acc.,
  come down, get down
[15] καροῦχα, ας, ἡ, carriage
[16] ἀποσύρω aor act inf, tear away,
  scrape off
[17] ἀντικνήμιον, ου, τό, shin
[18] προθύμως, adv, willingly, freely
[19] σπουδή, ῆς, ἡ, haste, speed
[20] στάδιον, ου, τό, stadium, arena
[21] θόρυβος, ου, ὁ, noise, clamor,
  confusion
[22] τηλικοῦτος, αύτη, οῦτο, so
  great, important
[23] στάδιον, ου, τό, stadium, arena
[24] Πολύκαρπος, ου, ὁ, Polycarp
[25] εἴσειμι pres act ptcp m.s.dat., go
  into
[26] στάδιον, ου, τό, stadium, arena
[27] ἰσχύω pres act impv 2s, have
  power, be mighty
[28] Πολύκαρπος, ου, ὁ, Polycarp
[29] ἀνδρίζομαι pres mid/pass impv
  2s, conduct oneself courageously

μὲν εἰπόντα οὐδεὶς εἶδεν, τὴν δὲ φωνὴν τῶν ἡμετέρων[1] οἱ παρόντες[2] ἤκουσαν. καὶ λοιπὸν προσαχθέντος[3] αὐτοῦ, θόρυβος[4] ἦν μέγας ἀκουσάντων, ὅτι Πολύκαρπος[5] συνείληπται.[6] **2** προσαχθέντα[7] οὖν αὐτὸν ἀνηρώτα[8] ὁ ἀνθύπατος,[9] εἰ αὐτὸς εἴη· Πολύκαρπος.[10] τοῦ δὲ ὁμολογοῦντος,[11] ἔπειθεν ἀρνεῖσθαι λέγων· Αἰδέσθητί[12] σου τὴν ἡλικίαν,[13] καὶ ἕτερα τούτοις ἀκόλουθα,[14] ὡς ἔθος[15] αὐτοῖς λέγειν· Ὄμοσον[16] τὴν Καίσαρος[17] τύχην,[18] μετανόησον, εἰπόν· Αἶρε τοὺς ἀθέους.[19] ὁ δὲ Πολύκαρπος[20] ἐμβριθεῖ[21] τῷ προσώπῳ εἰς πάντα τὸν ὄχλον τὸν ἐν τῷ σταδίῳ[22] ἀνόμων[23] ἐθνῶν ἐμβλέψας[24] καὶ ἐπισείσας[25] αὐτοῖς τὴν χεῖρα, στενάξας[26] τε καὶ ἀναβλέψας[27] εἰς τὸν οὐρανὸν εἶπεν· Αἶρε τοὺς ἀθέους.[28] **3** ἐγκειμένου[29] δὲ τοῦ ἀνθυπάτου[30] καὶ λέγοντος· Ὄμοσον,[31] καὶ ἀπολύω σε,

---

[1] ἡμέτερος, α, ον, our
[2] πάρειμι pres act ptcp m.p.nom., present
[3] προσάγω aor pass ptcp m.s.gen., bring (forward)
[4] θόρυβος, ου, ὁ, noise, clamor, confusion
[5] Πολύκαρπος, ου, ὁ, Polycarp
[6] συλλαμβάνω perf mid/pass ind 3s, seize, grasp, apprehend
[7] προσάγω aor pass ptcp m.s.acc., bring (forward)
[8] ἀνερωτάω aor act ind 3s, ask
[9] ἀνθύπατος, ου, ὁ, proconsul
[10] Πολύκαρπος, ου, ὁ, Polycarp
[11] ὁμολογέω pres act ptcp m.s.gen., admit, confess
[12] αἰδέομαι aor pass impv 2s, respect
[13] ἡλικία, ας, ἡ, age, time of life
[14] ἀκόλουθος, ον, following (sequence)
[15] ἔθος, ους, τό, habit, usage

[16] ὀμνύω aor act impv 2s, swear, take an oath
[17] Καῖσαρ, αρος, ὁ, caesar
[18] τύχη, ης, ἡ, fortune
[19] ἄθεος, ον, without God, athiest
[20] Πολύκαρπος, ου, ὁ, Polycarp
[21] ἐμβριθής, ές, dignified, serious
[22] στάδιον, ου, τό, stadium, arena
[23] ἄνομος, ον, lawless
[24] ἐμβλέπω aor act ptcp m.s.nom., look at, gaze on
[25] ἐπισείω aor act ptcp m.s.nom., shake at/against
[26] στενάζω aor act ptcp m.s.nom., sigh, groan
[27] ἀναβλέπω aor act ptcp m.s.nom., look up
[28] ἄθεος, ον, without God, atheist
[29] ἔγκειμαι pres mid/pass ptcp m.s.gen., insist, warn urgently
[30] ἀνθύπατος, ου, ὁ, proconsul
[31] ὀμνύω aor act impv 2s, swear, take an oath

λοιδόρησον[1] τὸν Χριστόν, ἔφη· ὁ Πολύκαρπος·[2] Ὀγδοήκοντα[3] καὶ ἓξ[4] ἔτη δουλεύω[5] αὐτῷ, καὶ οὐδέν με ἠδίκησεν·[6] καὶ πῶς δύναμαι βλασφημῆσαι τὸν βασιλέα μου τὸν σώσαντά με;

10:1 Ἐπιμένοντος[7] δὲ πάλιν αὐτοῦ καὶ λέγοντος· Ὅμοσον[8] τὴν Καίσαρος[9] τύχην,[10] ἀπεκρίνατο· Εἰ κενοδοξεῖς,[11] ἵνα ὀμόσω[12] τὴν καίσαρος[13] τύχην,[14] ὡς σὺ λέγεις, προσποιεῖ[15] δὲ ἀγνοεῖν[16] με, τίς εἰμι, μετὰ παρρησίας ἄκουε· Χριστιανός[17] εἰμι. εἰ δὲ θέλεις τὸν τοῦ Χριστιανισμοῦ[18] μαθεῖν[19] λόγον, δὸς ἡμέραν καὶ ἄκουσον. **2** ἔφη· ὁ ἀνθύπατος.[20] Πεῖσον τὸν δῆμον.[21] ὁ δὲ Πολύκαρπος[22] εἶπεν· Σὲ μὲν κἂν λόγου ἠξίωσα.[23] δεδιδάγμεθα γὰρ ἀρχαῖς καὶ ἐξουσίαις ὑπὸ θεοῦ τεταγμέναις[24] τιμὴν κατὰ τὸ προσῆκον,[25] τὴν μὴ βλάπτουσαν[26] ἡμᾶς, ἀπονέμειν·[27] ἐκείνους δὲ οὐκ ἀξίους ἡγοῦμαι[28] τοῦ ἀπολογεῖσθαι[29] αὐτοῖς.

---

[1] λοιδορέω aor act impv 2s, revile, abuse

[2] Πολύκαρπος, ου, ὁ, Polycarp

[3] ὀγδοήκοντα, eighty

[4] ἕξ, six

[5] δουλεύω pres act ind 1s, serve, obey

[6] ἀδικέω aor act ind 3s, do wrong

[7] ἐπιμένω pres act ptcp m.s.gen., continue, persist

[8] ὀμνύω aor act impv 2s, swear, take an oath

[9] Καῖσαρ, αρος, ὁ, caesar

[10] τύχη, ης, ἡ, fortune

[11] κενοδοξέω pres act ind 2s, vainly imagine

[12] ὀμνύω aor act sub 1s, swear, take an oath

[13] Καῖσαρ, αρος, ὁ, caesar

[14] τύχη, ης, ἡ, fortune

[15] προσποιέω pres act ind 3s, pretend

[16] ἀγνοέω pres act inf, not know, be ignorant (of)

[17] Χριστιανός, οῦ, ὁ, Christian

[18] Χριστιανισμός, οῦ, ὁ, Christianity

[19] μανθάνω aor act inf, learn

[20] ἀνθύπατος, ου, ὁ, proconsul

[21] δῆμος, ου, ὁ, people, crowd

[22] Πολύκαρπος, ου, ὁ, Polycarp

[23] ἀξιόω aor act ind 1s, consider worthy, deserving

[24] τάσσω perf mid/pass ptcp f.p.dat., arrange, put in place

[25] προσήκω pres act ptcp n.s.acc., suitable, proper

[26] βλάπτω pres act ptcp f.s.acc., harm, injure

[27] ἀπονέμω pres act inf, assign, show

[28] ἡγέομαι pres mid/pass ind 1s, lead, guide

[29] ἀπολογέομαι pres mid/pass inf, defend oneself

11:1 Ὁ δὲ ἀνθύπατος[1] εἶπεν· Θηρία ἔχω, τούτοις σε παραβαλῶ,[2] ἐὰν μὴ μετανοήσῃς. ὁ δὲ εἶπεν· Κάλει· ἀμετάθετος[3] γὰρ ἡμῖν ἡ ἀπὸ τῶν κρειττόνων[4] ἐπὶ τὰ χείρω[5] μετάνοια·[6] καλὸν δὲ μετατίθεσθαι[7] ἀπὸ τῶν χαλεπῶν[8] ἐπὶ τὰ δίκαια. **2** ὁ δὲ πάλιν πρὸς αὐτόν· Πυρί σε ποιήσω δαπανηθῆναι,[9] εἰ τῶν θηρίων καταφρονεῖς,[10] ἐὰν μὴ μετανοήσῃς. ὁ δὲ Πολύκαρπος[11] εἶπεν· Πῦρ ἀπειλεῖς[12] τὸ πρὸς ὥραν καιόμενον[13] καὶ μετ᾽ ὀλίγον σβεννύμενον·[14] ἀγνοεῖς[15] γὰρ τὸ τῆς μελλούσης κρίσεως καὶ αἰωνίου κολάσεως[16] τοῖς ἀσεβέσι[17] τηρούμενον πῦρ. ἀλλὰ τί βραδύνεις;[18] φέρε, ὃ βούλει.

12:1 Ταῦτα δὲ καὶ ἕτερα πλείονα λέγων θάρσους[19] καὶ χαρᾶς ἐνεπίμπλατο,[20] καὶ τὸ πρόσωπον αὐτοῦ χάριτος ἐπληροῦτο, ὥστε οὐ μόνον μὴ συμπεσεῖν[21] ταραχθέντα[22] ὑπὸ τῶν λεγομένων πρὸς αὐτόν, ἀλλὰ τοὐναντίον[23] τὸν ἀνθύπατον[24] ἐκστῆναι,[25] πέμψαι τε τὸν ἑαυτοῦ κήρυκα[26] ἐν μέσῳ τοῦ σταδίου[27] κηρύξαι

---

[1] ἀνθύπατος, ου, ὁ, proconsul
[2] παραβάλλω fut act ind 1s, throw to
[3] ἀμετάθετος, ον, impossible
[4] κρείττων, ον, higher in rank, better
[5] χείρων, ον, worse, more severe
[6] μετάνοια, ας, ἡ, repentance
[7] μετατίθημι pres mid/pass inf, change one's mind, turn away
[8] χαλεπός, ή, όν, hard, difficult
[9] δαπανάω aor pass inf, wear out, destroy
[10] καταφρονέω pres act ind 2s, care nothing for, disregard
[11] Πολύκαρπος, ου, ὁ, Polycarp
[12] ἀπειλέω pres act ind 2s, threaten, warn
[13] καίω pres mid/pass ptcp n.s.acc., keep burning
[14] σβέννυμι pres mid/pass ptcp n.s.acc., extinguish, put something out
[15] ἀγνοέω pres act ind 2s, not to know
[16] κόλασις, εως, ἡ, punishment
[17] ἀσεβής, ές, impious, ungodly
[18] βραδύνω pres act ind 2s, hesitate, delay
[19] θάρσος, ους, τό, courage
[20] ἐμπί(μ)πλημι imp mid/pass ind 3s, fill
[21] συμπίπτω aor act inf, collapse
[22] ταράσσω aor pass ptcp m.s.acc., unsettle, throw into confusion
[23] ἐναντίον, adv, on the other hand
[24] ἀνθύπατος, ου, ὁ, proconsul
[25] ἐξίστημι aor act inf, be amazed, be astonished
[26] κῆρυξ, υκος, ὁ, herald
[27] στάδιον, ου, τό, stadium, arena

τρίς.[1] Πολύκαρπος[2] ὡμολόγησεν[3] ἑαυτὸν Χριστιανὸν[4] εἶναι. 2 τούτου λεχθέντος ὑπὸ τοῦ κήρυκος,[5] ἅπαν τὸ πλῆθος ἐθνῶν τε καὶ Ἰουδαίων τῶν τὴν Σμύρναν[6] κατοικούντων ἀκατασχέτῳ[7] θυμῷ[8] καὶ μεγάλῃ φωνῇ ἐπεβόα.[9] Οὗτός ἐστιν ὁ τῆς Ἀσίας[10] διδάσκαλος, ὁ πατὴρ τῶν Χριστιανῶν,[11] ὁ τῶν ἡμετέρων[12] θεῶν καθαιρέτης,[13] ὁ πολλοὺς διδάσκων μὴ θύειν[14] μηδὲ προσκυνεῖν. ταῦτα λέγοντες ἐπεβόων[15] καὶ ἠρώτων τὸν Ἀσιάρχην[16] Φίλιππον, ἵνα ἐπαφῇ τῷ Πολυκάρπῳ[17] λέοντα.[18] ὁ δὲ ἔφη· μὴ εἶναι ἐξὸν αὐτῷ, ἐπειδὴ[19] πεπληρώκει τὰ κυνηγέσια.[20] 3 τότε ἔδοξεν αὐτοῖς ὁμοθυμαδὸν[21] ἐπιβοῆσαι,[22] ὥστε τὸν Πολύκαρπον[23] ζῶντα κατακαῦσαι.[24] ἔδει γὰρ τὸ τῆς φανερωθείσης αὐτῷ ἐπὶ τοῦ προσκεφαλαίου[25] ὀπτασίας[26] πληρωθῆναι, ὅτε ἰδὼν αὐτὸ καιόμενον[27] προσευχόμενος εἶπεν ἐπιστραφεὶς τοῖς σὺν αὐτῷ πιστοῖς προφητικῶς·[28] Δεῖ με ζῶντα καῆναι.[29]

---

[1] τρίς, adv, three times
[2] Πολύκαρπος, ου, ὁ, Polycarp
[3] ὁμολογέω aor act ind 3s, confess
[4] Χριστιανός, οῦ, ὁ, Christian
[5] κῆρυξ, υκος, ὁ, herald
[6] Σμύρνα, ης, ἡ, Smyrna
[7] ἀκατάσχετος, ον, uncontrollable
[8] θυμός, οῦ, ὁ, anger, rage
[9] ἐπιβοάω imp act ind 3s, cry out loudly
[10] Ἀσία, ας, ἡ, Asia
[11] Χριστιανός, οῦ, ὁ, Christian
[12] ἡμέτερος, α, ον, our
[13] καθαιρέτης, ου, ὁ, destroyer
[14] θύω pres act inf, sacrifice
[15] ἐπιβοάω imp act ind 3p, cry out loudly
[16] Ἀσιάρχης, ου, ὁ, Asiarch
[17] Πολύκαρπος, ου, ὁ, Polycarp

[18] λέων, οντος, ὁ, lion
[19] ἐπειδή, conj, since, because
[20] κυνηγέσιον, ου, τό, animal hunt
[21] ὁμοθυμαδόν, adv, together, with one mind
[22] ἐπιβοάω aor act inf, cry out loudly
[23] Πολύκαρπος, ου, ὁ, Polycarp
[24] κατακαίω aor act inf, burn up, consume
[25] προσκεφάλαιον, ου, τό, pillow, cushion
[26] ὀπτασία, ας, ἡ, vision, celestial sight
[27] καίω pres mid/pass ptcp n.s.acc., consumed, burn up
[28] προφητικῶς, adv, prophetically
[29] καίω pres mid/pass ptcp n.s.acc., consumed, burn up

13:1 Ταῦτα οὖν μετὰ τοσούτου[1] τάχους[2] ἐγένετο, θᾶττον[3] ἢ ἐλέγετο, τῶν ὄχλων παραχρῆμα[4] συναγόντων ἔκ τε τῶν ἐργαστηρίων[5] καὶ βαλανείων[6] ξύλα[7] καὶ φρύγανα,[8] μάλιστα[9] Ἰουδαίων προθύμως,[10] ὡς ἔθος[11] αὐτοῖς, εἰς ταῦτα ὑπουργούντων.[12] **2** ὅτε δὲ ἡ πυρκαϊὰ[13] ἡτοιμάσθη, ἀποθέμενος[14] ἑαυτῷ πάντα τὰ ἱμάτια καὶ λύσας τὴν ζώνην[15] ἐπειρᾶτο[16] καὶ ὑπολύειν[17] ἑαυτόν, μὴ πρότερον[18] τοῦτο ποιῶν διὰ τὸ ἀεὶ[19] ἕκαστον τῶν πιστῶν σπουδάζειν,[20] ὅστις τάχιον[21] τοῦ χρωτὸς[22] αὐτοῦ ἅψηται· παντὶ γὰρ καλῷ ἀγαθῆς ἕνεκεν πολιτείας[23] καὶ πρὸ τῆς μαρτυρίας ἐκεκόσμητο.[24] **3** εὐθέως οὖν αὐτῷ περιετίθετο[25] τὰ πρὸς τὴν πυρὰν[26] ἡρμοσμένα[27] ὄργανα.[28] μελλόντων δὲ αὐτῶν καὶ προσηλοῦν,[29] εἶπεν· Ἄφετέ με οὕτως· ὁ

---

[1] τοσοῦτος, αύτη, οῦτον, so great, so strong
[2] τάχος, ους, τό, speed, swiftness
[3] ταχέως, adv, with haste, quickly
[4] παραχρῆμα, adv, immediately
[5] ἐργαστήριον, ίου, τό, workshop
[6] βαλανεῖον, ου, τό, bathhouse
[7] ξύλον, ου, τό, wood
[8] φρύγανον, ου, τό, brushwood
[9] μάλιστα, adv, most of all, especially
[10] προθύμως, adv, willingly, eagerly
[11] ἔθος, ους, τό, habit, custom
[12] ὑπουργέω pres act ptcp m.p.gen., be helpful, assist
[13] πυρκαϊά, ᾶς, ἡ, funeral pyre
[14] ἀποτίθημι aor mid ptcp m.s.nom., take off
[15] ζώνη, ης, ἡ, belt
[16] πειράω imp mid/pass ind 3s, try, attempt

[17] ὑπολύω pres act inf, take off one's shoes
[18] πρότερος, α, ον, formerly
[19] ἀεί, adv, constantly, continually
[20] σπουδάζω pres act inf, hurry, hasten
[21] ταχέως, adv, faster, quicker
[22] χρώς, χρωτός, ὁ, skin
[23] πολιτεία, ας, ἡ, way of life, conduct
[24] κοσμέω plupf mid/pass ind 3s, adorn, decorate
[25] περιτίθημι imp mid/pass ind 3s, place around
[26] πυρά, ᾶς, ἡ, fire, pyre
[27] ἁρμόζω perf mid/pass ptcp n.p.acc., join
[28] ὄργανον, ου, τό, tool
[29] προσηλόω pres act inf, nail

27

γὰρ δοὺς ὑπομεῖναι[1] τὸ πῦρ δώσει καὶ χωρὶς τῆς ὑμετέρας[2] ἐκ τῶν ἥλων[3] ἀσφαλείας[4] ἄσκυλτον[5] ἐπιμεῖναι[6] τῇ πυρᾷ.[7]

14:1 Οἱ δὲ οὐ καθήλωσαν[8] μέν, προσέδησαν[9] δὲ αὐτόν. ὁ δὲ ὀπίσω τὰς χεῖρας ποιήσας καὶ προσδεθείς,[10] ὥσπερ κριὸς[11] ἐπίσημος[12] ἐκ μεγάλου ποιμνίου[13] εἰς προσφοράν,[14] ὁλο-καύτωμα[15] δεκτὸν[16] τῷ θεῷ ἡτοιμασμένον, ἀναβλέψας[17] εἰς τὸν οὐρανὸν εἶπεν· Κύριε ὁ θεὸς ὁ παντοκράτωρ,[18] ὁ τοῦ ἀγαπητοῦ καὶ εὐλογητοῦ[19] παιδός[20] σου Ἰησοῦ Χριστοῦ πατήρ, δι' οὗ τὴν περὶ σοῦ ἐπίγνωσιν[21] εἰλήφαμεν, ὁ θεὸς ἀγγέλων καὶ δυνάμεων καὶ πάσης τῆς κτίσεως,[22] παντός τε τοῦ γένους[23] τῶν δικαίων, οἳ ζῶσιν ἐνώπιόν σου· **2** εὐλογῶ σε, ὅτι ἠξίωσάς[24] με τῆς ἡμέρας καὶ ὥρας ταύτης, τοῦ λαβεῖν με μέρος ἐν ἀριθμῷ[25] τῶν μαρτύρων ἐν τῷ ποτηρίῳ τοῦ Χριστοῦ σου εἰς ἀνάστασιν ζωῆς αἰωνίου ψυχῆς τε καὶ σώματος ἐν ἀφθαρσίᾳ[26] πνεύματος ἁγίου· ἐν οἷς προσδεχθείην[27] ἐνώπιόν σου σήμερον ἐν θυσίᾳ[28] πίονι[29] καὶ

---

[1] ὑπομένω aor act inf, endure
[2] ὑμέτερος, α, ον, belong to
[3] ἧλος, ου, ὁ, nail
[4] ἀσφάλεια, ας, ἡ, security
[5] ἄσκυλτος, ον, unmoved
[6] ἐπιμένω aor act inf, remain
[7] πυρά, ᾶς, ἡ, fire, pyre
[8] καθηλόω aor act ind 3p, fasten with nails
[9] προσδέω aor act ind 3p, tie, bind
[10] προσδέω aor pass ptcp m.s.nom., tie, bind
[11] κριός, οῦ, ὁ, male sheep, ram
[12] ἐπίσημος, ον, splendid
[13] ποίμνιον, ου, τό, flock
[14] προσφορά, ᾶς, ἡ, offering
[15] ὁλοκαύτωμα, ατος, τό, burnt offering
[16] δεκτός, ή, όν, pleasing, acceptable
[17] ἀναβλέπω aor act ptcp m.s.nom., look up
[18] παντοκράτωρ, ορος, ὁ, Almighty
[19] εὐλογητός, ή, όν, blessed
[20] παῖς, παιδός, ὁ, servant
[21] ἐπίγνωσις, εως, ἡ, knowledge
[22] κτίσις, εως, ἡ, creation
[23] γένος, ους, τό, nation, people
[24] ἀξιόω aor act ind 2s, consider worthy
[25] ἀριθμός, οῦ, ὁ, number
[26] ἀφθαρσία, ας, ἡ, incorruptibility, immortal
[27] προσδέχομαι aor pass opt 1s, receive in a friendly manner
[28] θυσία, ας, ἡ, sacrifice, offering
[29] πίων, πῖον, fat

προσδεκτῇ,¹ καθὼς προητοίμασας² καὶ προεφανέρωσας³ καὶ
ἐπλήρωσας, ὁ ἀψευδὴς⁴ καὶ ἀληθινὸς⁵ θεός. **3** διὰ τοῦτο καὶ περὶ
πάντων σὲ αἰνῶ,⁶ σὲ εὐλογῶ, σὲ δοξάζω διὰ τοῦ αἰωνίου καὶ
ἐπουρανίου⁷ ἀρχιερέως Ἰησοῦ Χριστοῦ, ἀγαπητοῦ σου παιδός,⁸
δι' οὗ σοὶ σὺν αὐτῷ καὶ πνεύματι ἁγίῳ δόξα καὶ νῦν καὶ εἰς τοὺς
μέλλοντας αἰῶνας. ἀμήν.

15:1 Ἀναπέμψαντος⁹ δὲ αὐτοῦ τὸ ἀμὴν καὶ πληρώσαντος τὴν
εὐχήν,¹⁰ οἱ τοῦ πυρὸς ἄνθρωποι ἐξῆψαν¹¹ τὸ πῦρ. μεγάλης δὲ
ἐκλαμψάσης¹² φλογός,¹³ θαῦμα¹⁴ εἴδομεν, οἷς ἰδεῖν ἐδόθη· οἳ καὶ
ἐτηρήθημεν εἰς τὸ ἀναγγεῖλαι¹⁵ τοῖς λοιποῖς τὰ γενόμενα. **2** τὸ
γὰρ πῦρ καμάρας¹⁶ εἶδος¹⁷ ποιῆσαν, ὥσπερ ὀθόνη.¹⁸ πλοίου ὑπὸ
πνεύματος πληρουμένη, κύκλῳ¹⁹ περιετείχισεν²⁰ τὸ σῶμα τοῦ
μάρτυρος· καὶ ἦν μέσον οὐχ ὡς σὰρξ καιομένη²¹ ἀλλ' ὡς ἄρτος
ὀπτώμενος²² ἢ ὡς χρυσὸς²³ καὶ ἄργυρος²⁴ ἐν καμίνῳ²⁵

---

¹ προσδεκτός, ή, όν, acceptable
² προετοιμάζω aor act ind 2s,
  prepare beforehand
³ προφανερόω aor act ind 2s, reveal
  beforehand
⁴ ἀψευδής, ές, trustworthy, truthful
⁵ ἀληθινός, ή, όν, true, trustworthy
⁶ αἰνέω pres act ind 1s, praise
⁷ ἐπουράνιος, ον, heaven, heavenly
⁸ παῖς, παιδός, ὁ, servant
⁹ ἀναπέμπω aor act ptcp m.s.gen.,
  send up
¹⁰ εὐχή, ῆς, ἡ, prayer
¹¹ ἐξάπτω aor act ind 3p, set fire,
  kindle
¹² ἐκλάμπω aor act ptcp f.s.gen.,
  shine forth
¹³ φλόξ, φλογός, ἡ, flame

¹⁴ θαῦμα, ατος, τό, miracle
¹⁵ ἀναγγέλλω aor act inf, disclose,
  report
¹⁶ καμάρα, ας, ἡ, arch
¹⁷ εἶδος, ους, τό, form, outward
  appearance
¹⁸ ὀθόνη, ης, ἡ, linen cloth, sheet
¹⁹ κύκλῳ, adv, around
²⁰ περιτειχίζω aor act ind 3s,
  surround
²¹ καίω pres mid/pass ptcp f.s.nom.,
  burn up
²² ὀπτάω pres mid/pass ptcp
  m.s.nom., bake
²³ χρυσός, οῦ, ὁ, gold
²⁴ ἄργυρος, ου, ὁ, silver
²⁵ κάμινος, ου, ἡ, furnace

πυρούμενος.¹ καὶ γὰρ εὐωδίας² τοσαύτης³ ἀντελαβόμεθα,⁴ ὡς λιβανωτοῦ⁵ πνέοντος⁶ ἢ ἄλλου τινὸς τῶν τιμίων⁷ ἀρωμάτων.⁸

16:1 Πέρας⁹ γοῦν¹⁰ ἰδόντες οἱ ἄνομοι¹¹ μὴ δυνάμενον αὐτοῦ τὸ σῶμα ὑπὸ τοῦ πυρὸς δαπανηθῆναι,¹² ἐκέλευσαν¹³ προσελθόντα αὐτῷ κομφέκτορα¹⁴ παραβῦσαι¹⁵ ξιφίδιον.¹⁶ καὶ τοῦτο ποιήσαντος, ἐξῆλθεν περιστερὰ¹⁷ καὶ πλῆθος αἵματος, ὥστε κατασβέσαι¹⁸ τὸ πῦρ καὶ θαυμάσαι πάντα τὸν ὄχλον, εἰ τοσαύτη¹⁹ τις διαφορὰ²⁰ μεταξὺ²¹ τῶν τε ἀπίστων²² καὶ τῶν ἐκλεκτῶν·²³ **2** ὧν εἷς καὶ οὗτος γεγόνει ὁ θαυμασιώτατος²⁴ μάρτυς Πολύκαρπος,²⁵ ἐν τοῖς καθ᾽ ἡμᾶς χρόνοις διδάσκαλος ἀποστολικὸς²⁶ καὶ προφητικὸς²⁷ γενόμενος, ἐπίσκοπος²⁸ τῆς ἐν Σμύρνῃ²⁹ καθολικῆς³⁰ ἐκκλησίας. πᾶν γὰρ ῥῆμα, ὃ ἀφῆκεν ἐκ τοῦ στόματος αὐτοῦ, ἐτελειώθη.³¹ καὶ τελειωθήσεται.³²

---

¹ πυρόω pres mid/pass ptcp m.s.nom., heat thoroughly
² εὐωδία, ας, ἡ, aroma, fragrance
³ τοσοῦτος, αύτη, οῦτον, so great
⁴ ἀντιλαμβάνω aor mid ind 1p, perceive, notice
⁵ λιβανωτός, οῦ, ὁ, incense
⁶ πνέω pres act ptcp m.s.gen., breathe out
⁷ τίμιος, α, ον, costly, precious
⁸ ἄρωμα, ατος, τό, fragrant spice
⁹ πέρας, ατος, τό, finally, in conclusion
¹⁰ γοῦν, part, then
¹¹ ἄνομος, ον, lawless
¹² δαπανάω aor pass inf, wear out, destroy
¹³ κελεύω aor act ind 3p, command, urge
¹⁴ κομφέκτωρ, ορος, ὁ, executioner
¹⁵ παραβύω aor act inf, plunge into

¹⁶ ξιφίδιον, ου, τό, short sword, dagger
¹⁷ περιστερά, ᾶς, ἡ, dove
¹⁸ κατασβέννυμι aor act inf, put out, quench
¹⁹ τοσοῦτος, αύτη, οῦτον, so great
²⁰ διαφορά, ᾶς, ἡ, difference
²¹ μεταξύ, adv, between
²² ἄπιστος, ον, unbelieving
²³ ἐκλεκτός, ή, όν, elect
²⁴ θαυμάσιος, α, ον, remarkable
²⁵ Πολύκαρπος, ου, ὁ, Polycarp
²⁶ ἀποστολικός, ή, όν, apostolic
²⁷ προφητικός, ή, όν, prophetic
²⁸ ἐπίσκοπος, ου, ὁ, bishop
²⁹ Σμύρνα, ης, ἡ, Smyrna
³⁰ καθολικός, ή, όν, general, universal
³¹ τελειόω aor pass ind 3s, fulfill, accomplish
³² τελειόω fut pass ind 3s, fulfill, accomplish

17:1 Ὁ δὲ ἀντίζηλος[1] καὶ βάσκανος[2] καὶ πονηρός, ὁ ἀντικείμενος[3] τῷ γένει[4] τῶν δικαίων, ἰδὼν τό τε μέγεθος[5] αὐτοῦ τῆς μαρτυρίας καὶ τὴν ἀπ’ ἀρχῆς ἀνεπίληπτον[6] πολιτείαν,[7] ἐστεφανωμένον[8] τε τὸν τῆς ἀφθαρσίας[9] στέφανον[10] καὶ βραβεῖον[11] ἀναντίρρητον[12] ἀπενηνεγμένον,[13] ἐπετήδευσεν,[14] ὡς μηδὲ τὸ σωμάτιον[15] αὐτοῦ ὑφ’ ἡμῶν ληφθῆναι, καίπερ[16] πολλῶν ἐπιθυμούντων[17] τοῦτο ποιῆσαι καὶ κοινωνῆσαι[18] τῷ ἁγίῳ αὐτοῦ σαρκίῳ.[19] **2** ὑπέβαλεν[20] γοῦν[21] Νικήτην[22] τὸν τοῦ Ἡρώδου πατέρα, ἀδελφὸν δὲ Ἄλκης,[23] ἐντυχεῖν[24] τῷ ἄρχοντι, ὥστε μὴ δοῦναι αὐτοῦ τὸ σῶμα· μή, φησίν, ἀφέντες τὸν ἐσταυρωμένον τοῦτον ἄρξωνται σέβεσθαι.[25] καὶ ταῦτα εἶπον ὑποβαλλόντων[26] καὶ ἐνισχυόντων[27] τῶν Ἰουδαίων, οἳ καὶ ἐτήρησαν, μελλόντων ἡμῶν ἐκ τοῦ πυρὸς αὐτὸν λαμβάνειν· ἀγνοοῦντες,[28] ὅτι οὔτε τὸν Χριστόν ποτε[29] καταλιπεῖν[30] δυνησόμεθα, τὸν ὑπὲρ τῆς τοῦ παντὸς κόσμου τῶν σῳζομένων σωτηρίας παθόντα ἄμωμον[31]

---

[1] ἀντίζηλος, ου, ὁ, jealous one
[2] βάσκανος, ου, ὁ, envious one
[3] ἀντίκειμαι pres mid/pass ptcp m.s.nom., be in opposition to
[4] γένος, ους, τό, race, people
[5] μέγεθος, ους, τό, greatness
[6] ἀνεπίλη(μ)πτος, ον, irreproachable
[7] πολιτεία, ας, ἡ, way of life, conduct
[8] στεφανόω perf mid/pass ptcp m.s.acc., crown, reward
[9] ἀφθαρσία, ας, ἡ, immortality
[10] στέφανος, ου, ὁ, crown
[11] βραβεῖον, ου, τό, prize, award
[12] ἀναντίρρητος, ον, undeniable, not to be contradicted
[13] ἀποφέρω perf mid/pass ptcp m.s.acc., carry off, win
[14] ἐπιτηδεύω aor act ind 3s, take care
[15] σωμάτιον, ου, τό, poor body

[16] καίπερ, conj, although
[17] ἐπιθυμέω pres act ptcp m.p.gen., desire, long for
[18] κοινωνέω aor act inf, share
[19] σαρκίον, ου, τό, piece of flesh
[20] ὑποβάλλω aor act ind 3s, instigate
[21] γοῦν, part, then
[22] Νικήτης, ου, Nicetes
[23] Ἄλκη, ης, ἡ, Alce
[24] ἐντυγχάνω aor act inf, approach
[25] σέβω pres mid/pass inf, worship
[26] ὑποβάλλω pres act ptcp m.p.gen., instigate
[27] ἐνισχύω pres act ptcp m.p.gen., strengthen
[28] ἀγνοέω pres act ptcp m.p.nom., be ignorant
[29] ποτέ, adv, some time
[30] καταλείπω aor act inf, leave behind
[31] ἄμωμος, ον, blameless

31

ὑπὲρ ἁμαρτωλῶν, οὔτε ἕτερόν τινα σέβεσθαι.[1] **3** τοῦτον μὲν γὰρ υἱὸν ὄντα τοῦ θεοῦ προσκυνοῦμεν, τοὺς δὲ μάρτυρας ὡς μαθητὰς καὶ μιμητὰς[2] τοῦ κυρίου ἀγαπῶμεν ἀξίως[3] ἕνεκεν[4] εὐνοίας[5] ἀνυπερβλήτου[6] τῆς εἰς τὸν ἴδιον βασιλέα καὶ διδάσκαλον· ὧν γένοιτο καὶ ἡμᾶς κοινωνούς[7] τε καὶ συμμαθητὰς[8] γενέσθαι.

18:1 Ἰδὼν οὖν ὁ κεντυρίων[9] τὴν τῶν Ἰουδαίων γενομένην φιλονεικίαν,[10] θεὶς αὐτὸν ἐν μέσῳ, ὡς ἔθος[11] αὐτοῖς, ἔκαυσεν.[12] **2** οὕτως τε ἡμεῖς ὕστερον[13] ἀνελόμενοι[14] τὰ τιμιώτερα[15] λίθων πολυτελῶν[16] καὶ δοκιμώτερα[17] ὑπὲρ χρυσίον[18] ὀστᾶ[19] αὐτοῦ ἀπεθέμεθα,[20] ὅπου καὶ ἀκόλουθον[21] ἦν. **3** ἔνθα[22] ὡς δυνατὸν ἡμῖν συναγομένοις ἐν ἀγαλλιάσει[23] καὶ χαρᾷ· παρέξει[24] ὁ κύριος ἐπιτελεῖν[25] τὴν τοῦ μαρτυρίου[26] αὐτοῦ ἡμέραν γενέθλιον,[27] εἴς τε τὴν τῶν προηθληκότων[28] μνήμην[29] καὶ τῶν μελλόντων ἄσκησίν[30] τε καὶ ἑτοιμασίαν.[31]

---

[1] σέβω pres mid/pass inf, worship

[2] μιμητής, οῦ, ὁ, imitator

[3] ἀξίως, adv, worthily

[4] ἕνεκα, prep, on account of

[5] εὔνοια, ας, ἡ, favor, affection

[6] ἀνυπέρβλητος, ον, unsurpassable, unexcelled

[7] κοινωνός, οῦ, ὁ, participant, partner

[8] συμμαθητής, οῦ, ὁ, fellow-disciple

[9] κεντυρίων, ωνος, ὁ, centurion

[10] φιλονεικία, ας, ἡ, contentiousness

[11] ἔθος, ους, τό, habit, custom

[12] καίω aor act ind 3s, burn up

[13] ὕστερος, α, ον, later, thereafter

[14] ἀναιρέω aor mid ptcp m.p.nom., take up, claim for oneself

[15] τίμιος, α, ον, honor

[16] πολυτελής, ές, costly, expensive

[17] δόκιμος, ον, precious

[18] χρυσίον, ου, τό, gold

[19] ὀστέον, ου, bone

[20] ἀποτίθημι aor mid ind 1p, put away, lay down

[21] ἀκόλουθος, ον, following (sequence)

[22] ἔνθα, adv, there

[23] ἀγαλλίασις, εως, ἡ, exultation

[24] παρέχω fut act ind 3s, present, offer

[25] ἐπιτελέω pres act inf, fulfill, complete

[26] μαρτύριον, ου, τό, martyrdom

[27] γενέθλιος, ον, birthday

[28] προαθλέω perf act ptcp m.p.gen., compete in former times

[29] μνήμη, ης, ἡ, memory, remembrance

[30] ἄσκησις, εως, ἡ, practice

[31] ἑτοιμασία, ας, ἡ, readiness, preparation

19:1 Τοιαῦτα τὰ κατὰ τὸν μακάριον Πολύκαρπον,[1] ὃς σὺν τοῖς ἀπὸ Φιλαδελφίας[2] δωδέκατος[3] ἐν Σμύρνῃ[4] μαρτυρήσας, μόνος ὑπὸ πάντων μᾶλλον μνημονεύεται,[5] ὥστε καὶ ὑπὸ τῶν ἐθνῶν ἐν παντὶ τόπῳ λαλεῖσθαι· οὐ μόνον διδάσκαλος γενόμενος ἐπίσημος,[6] ἀλλὰ καὶ μάρτυς ἔξοχος,[7] οὗ τὸ μαρτύριον[8] πάντες ἐπιθυμοῦσιν[9] μιμεῖσθαι[10] κατὰ τὸ εὐαγγέλιον Χριστοῦ γενόμενον. **2** διὰ τῆς ὑπομονῆς καταγωνισάμενος[11] τὸν ἄδικον[12] ἄρχοντα καὶ οὕτως τὸν τῆς ἀφθαρσίας[13] στέφανον[14] ἀπολαβών,[15] σὺν τοῖς ἀποστόλοις καὶ πᾶσιν δικαίοις ἀγαλλιώμενος[16] δοξάζει τὸν θεὸν καὶ πατέρα παντοκράτορα[17] καὶ εὐλογεῖ τὸν κύριον ἡμῶν Ἰησοῦν Χριστόν, τὸν σωτῆρα[18] τῶν ψυχῶν ἡμῶν καὶ κυβερνήτην[19] τῶν σωμάτων ἡμῶν καὶ ποιμένα[20] τῆς κατὰ τὴν οἰκουμένην[21] καθολικῆς[22] ἐκκλησίας.

20:1 Ὑμεῖς μὲν οὖν ἠξιώσατε[23] διὰ πλειόνων δηλωθῆναι[24] ὑμῖν τὰ γενόμενα, ἡμεῖς δὲ κατὰ τὸ παρὸν[25] ἐπὶ κεφαλαίῳ[26]

---

[1] Πολύκαρπος, ου, ὁ, Polycarp
[2] φιλαδελφία, ας, ἡ, Philadelphia
[3] δωδέκατος, η, ον, twelfth
[4] Σμύρνα, ης, ἡ, Smyrna
[5] μνημονεύω pres mid/pass ind 3s, remember
[6] ἐπίσημος, ον, prominent, outstanding
[7] ἔξοχος, ον, punishment
[8] μαρτύριον, ου, τό, martyrdom
[9] ἐπιθυμέω pres act ind 3p, desire, long for
[10] μιμέομαι pres mid/pass inf, imitate
[11] καταγωνίζομαι aor mid ptcp m.s.nom., conquer, defeat
[12] ἄδικος, ον, unjust
[13] ἀφθαρσία, ας, ἡ, incorruptibility, immortality

[14] στέφανος, ου, ὁ, prize, reward
[15] ἀπολαμβάνω aor act ptcp m.s.nom., receive
[16] ἀγαλλιάω pres mid/pass ptcp m.s.nom., be glad, rejoice
[17] παντοκράτωρ, ορος, ὁ, Almighty
[18] σωτήρ, ῆρος, ὁ, savior
[19] κυβερνήτης, ου, ὁ, pilot
[20] ποιμήν, ένος, ὁ, shepherd
[21] οἰκουμένη, ης, ἡ, world
[22] καθολικός, ή, όν, general, universal
[23] ἀξιόω aor act ind 2p, worthy
[24] δηλόω aor pass inf, reveal, make clear
[25] πάρειμι pres act ptcp n.s.acc., be present
[26] κεφάλαιον, ου, τό, main point

μεμηνύκαμεν[1] διὰ τοῦ ἀδελφοῦ ἡμῶν Μαρκίωνος.[2] μαθόντες[3] οὖν ταῦτα καὶ τοῖς ἐπέκεινα[4] ἀδελφοῖς τὴν ἐπιστολὴν διαπέμψασθε,[5] ἵνα καὶ ἐκεῖνοι δοξάζωσιν τὸν κύριον τὸν ἐκλογὰς[6] ποιοῦντα ἀπὸ τῶν ἰδίων δούλων. 2 τῷ δὲ δυναμένῳ πάντας ἡμᾶς εἰσαγαγεῖν[7] ἐν τῇ αὐτοῦ χάριτι καὶ δωρεᾷ[8] εἰς τὴν ἐπουράνιον[9] αὐτοῦ βασιλείαν διὰ τοῦ μονογενοῦς[10] παιδὸς[11] αὐτοῦ Ἰησοῦ Χριστοῦ, δόξα, τιμή, κράτος,[12] μεγαλωσύνη·[13] εἰς τοὺς αἰῶνας. προσαγορεύετε[14] πάντας τοὺς ἁγίους. ὑμᾶς οἱ σὺν ἡμῖν προσαγορεύουσιν[15] καὶ Εὔαρεστος[16] ὁ γράψας πανοικεί.[17]

21:1 Μαρτυρεῖ δὲ ὁ μακάριος Πολύκαρπος[18] μηνὸς[19] Ξανθικοῦ[20] δευτέρᾳ ἱσταμένου, πρὸ ἑπτὰ καλανδῶν[21] Μαρτίων,[22] σαββάτῳ μεγάλῳ, ὥρᾳ ὀγδόη.[23] συνελήφθη·[24] δὲ ὑπὸ Ἡρώδου ἐπὶ ἀρχιερέως Φιλίππου Τραλλιανοῦ,[25] ἀνθυπατεύοντος[26] Στατίου[27] Κοδράτου,[28] βασιλεύοντος[29] δὲ εἰς τοὺς αἰῶνας Ἰησοῦ Χριστοῦ· ᾧ ἡ δόξα, τιμή, μεγαλωσύνη·[30] θρόνος αἰώνιος ἀπὸ γενεᾶς εἰς γενεάν. ἀμήν.

---

[1] μηνύω perf act ind 1p, inform
[2] Μαρκίων, ωνος, ὁ, Marcion
[3] μανθάνω aor act ptcp m.p.nom., learn
[4] ἐπέκεινα, adv, beyond
[5] διαπέμπω aor mid impv 2p, send on
[6] ἐκλογή, ῆς, ἡ, selection, election
[7] εἰσάγω aor act inf, bring, lead into
[8] δωρεά, ᾶς, ἡ, bounty, gift
[9] ἐπουράνιος, ον, heavenly
[10] μονογενής, ές, unique, begotten
[11] παῖς, παιδός, ὁ, servant
[12] κράτος, ους, τό, power
[13] μεγαλωσύνη, ης, ἡ, majesty
[14] προσαγορεύω pres act impv 2p, greet
[15] προσαγορεύω pres act ind 3p, greet
[16] Εὔαρεστος, ου, ὁ, Evarestus
[17] πανοικεί/πανοικί (πᾶς + οἶκος), one's whole household
[18] Πολύκαρπος, ου, ὁ, Polycarp
[19] μήν, μηνός, ὁ, month
[20] Ξανθικός, ου, ὁ, Xanthicus
[21] καλάνδαι, ῶν, αἱ, calends
[22] Μάρτιος, ίου, ὁ, March
[23] ὄγδοος, η, ον, eighth
[24] συλλαμβάνω aor pass ind 3s, seize, grasp
[25] Τραλλιανός, οῦ, ὁ, Tralles
[26] ἀνθυπατεύω pres act ptcp m.s.gen., be proconsul
[27] Στάτιος, ου, ὁ, Statius
[28] Κοδράτος, ου, ὁ, Quadratus
[29] βασιλεύω pres act ptcp m.s.gen., reign
[30] μεγαλωσύνη, ης, ἡ, majesty

22:1 Ἐρρῶσθαι[1] ὑμᾶς εὐχόμεθα,[2] ἀδελφοί, στοιχοῦντας[3] τῷ κατὰ τὸ εὐαγγέλιον λόγῳ Ἰησοῦ Χριστοῦ, μεθ' οὗ δόξα τῷ θεῷ καὶ πατρὶ καὶ ἁγίῳ πνεύματι, ἐπὶ σωτηρίᾳ τῇ τῶν ἁγίων ἐκλεκτῶν,[4] καθὼς ἐμαρτύρησεν ὁ μακάριος Πολύκαρπος,[5] οὗ γένοιτο ἐν τῇ βασιλείᾳ Ἰησοῦ Χριστοῦ πρὸς τὰ ἴχνη·[6] εὑρεθῆναι ἡμᾶς.

22:2 Ταῦτα μετεγράψατο[7] μὲν Γάϊος[8] ἐκ τῶν Εἰρηναίου,[9] μαθητοῦ τοῦ Πολυκάρπου, ὃς καὶ συνεπολιτεύσατο[10] τῷ Εἰρηναίῳ.[11] ἐγὼ δὲ Σωκράτης[12] ἐν Κορίνθῳ[13] ἐκ τῶν Γαΐου[14] ἀντιγράφων[15] ἔγραψα. ἡ χάρις μετὰ πάντων.

22:3 Ἐγὼ δὲ πάλιν Πιόνιος[16] ἐκ τοῦ προγεγραμμένου[17] ἔγραψα ἀναζητήσας[18] αὐτά, κατὰ ἀποκάλυψιν[19] φανερώσαντός μοι τοῦ μακαρίου Πολυκάρπου,[20] καθὼς δηλώσω[21] ἐν τῷ καθεξῆς,[22] συναγαγὼν αὐτὰ ἤδη σχεδὸν[23] ἐκ τοῦ χρόνου κεκμηκότα,[24] ἵνα κἀμὲ συναγάγῃ ὁ κύριος Ἰησοῦς Χριστὸς μετὰ τῶν ἐκλεκτῶν[25]

---

[1] ῥώννυμι perf mid/pass inf, goodbye, be strengthened

[2] εὔχομαι pres mid/pass ind 1p, wish

[3] στοιχέω pres act ptcp m.p.acc., agree, conform

[4] ἐκλεκτός, ή, όν, selected, chosen

[5] Πολύκαρπος, ου, ὁ, Polycarp

[6] ἴχνος, ους, τό, footprint

[7] μεταγράφω aor mid ind 3s, copy, transcribe

[8] Γάϊος, ου, ὁ, Gaius

[9] Εἰρηναῖος, ου, ὁ, Irenaeus

[10] συμπολιτεύομαι aor mid ind 3s, be a fellow citizen

[11] Εἰρηναῖος, ου, ὁ, Irenaeus

[12] Σωκράτης, ους, ὁ, Socrates

[13] Κόρινθος, ου, ἡ, Corinth

[14] Γάϊος, ου, ὁ, Gaius

[15] ἀντίγραφον, ου, τό, copy

[16] Πιόνιος, ου, ὁ, Pionius

[17] προγράφω perf mid/pass ptcp n.s.gen., write beforehand

[18] ἀναζητέω aor act ptcp m.s.nom., look, search

[19] ἀποκάλυψις, εως, ἡ, revelation

[20] Πολύκαρπος, ου, ὁ, Polycarp

[21] δηλόω fut act ind 1s, reveal, make clear

[22] καθεξῆς, adv, in order, one after the other

[23] σχεδόν, adv, nearly, almost

[24] κάμνω perf act ptcp m.s.acc., weary, fatigued

[25] ἐκλεκτός, ή, όν, chosen, elect

αὐτοῦ εἰς τὴν οὐράνιον¹ βασιλείαν αὐτοῦ, ᾧ ἡ δόξα σὺν πατρὶ καὶ ἁγίῳ πνεύματι εἰς τοὺς αἰῶνας τῶν αἰώνων, ἀμήν.

23:1 (22.2) Ταῦτα μετεγράψατο² μὲν Γάϊος³ ἐκ τῶν Εἰρηναίου⁴ συγγραμμάτων,⁵ ὃς καὶ συνεπολιτεύσατο⁶ τῷ Εἰρηναίῳ,⁷ μαθητῇ γεγονότι τοῦ ἁγίου Πολυκάρπου.⁸ οὗτος γὰρ ὁ Εἰρηναῖος,⁹ κατὰ τὸν καιρὸν τοῦ μαρτυρίου¹⁰ τοῦ ἐπισκόπου¹¹ Πολυκάρπου¹² γενόμενος ἐν Ῥώμῃ,¹³ πολλοὺς ἐδίδαξεν· οὗ καὶ πολλὰ αὐτοῦ συγγράμματα¹⁴ κάλλιστα καὶ ὀρθότατα¹⁵ φέρεται· ἐν οἷς μέμνηται¹⁶ Πολυκάρπου,¹⁷ ὅτι παρ' αὐτοῦ ἔμαθεν.¹⁸ ἱκανῶς¹⁹ τε πᾶσαν αἵρεσιν²⁰ ἤλεγξεν²¹ καὶ τὸν ἐκκλησιαστικὸν²² κανόνα²³ καὶ καθολικόν,²⁴ ὡς παρέλαβεν παρὰ τοῦ ἁγίου, καὶ παρέδωκεν. λέγει δὲ καὶ τοῦτο, ὅτι συναντήσαντός²⁵ ποτε²⁶ τῷ ἁγίῳ Πολυκάρπῳ²⁷ Μαρκίωνος,²⁸ ἀφ' οὗ οἱ λεγόμενοι Μαρκιωνισταί,²⁹ καὶ εἰπόντος· Ἐπιγίνωσκε ἡμᾶς, Πολύ-καρπε,³⁰ εἶπεν αὐτὸς τῷ Μαρκίωνι.³¹ Ἐπιγινώσκω, ἐπιγινώσκω τὸν πρωτότοκον³² τοῦ σατανᾶ. καὶ τοῦτο δὲ φέρεται ἐν τοῖς τοῦ

¹ οὐράνιος, ον, heavenly
² μεταγράφω aor mid ind 3s, copy
³ Γάϊος, ου, ὁ, Gaius
⁴ Εἰρηναῖος, ου, ὁ, Irenaeus
⁵ σύγγραμμα, ατος, τό, book, written work
⁶ συμπολιτεύομαι aor mid ind 3s, fellow citizen
⁷ Εἰρηναῖος, ου, ὁ, Irenaeus
⁸ Πολύκαρπος, ου, ὁ, Polycarp
⁹ Εἰρηναῖος, ου, ὁ, Irenaeus
¹⁰ μαρτύριον, ου, τό, martyrdom
¹¹ ἐπίσκοπος, ου, ὁ, bishop
¹² Πολύκαρπος, ου, ὁ, Polycarp
¹³ Ῥώμη, ης, ἡ, Rome
¹⁴ σύγγραμμα, ατος, τό, book, written work
¹⁵ ὀρθός, ή, όν, correct, orthodox
¹⁶ μιμνήσκομαι perf mid/pass ind 3s, remember
¹⁷ Πολύκαρπος, ου, ὁ, Polycarp
¹⁸ μανθάνω aor act ind 3s, learn
¹⁹ ἱκανῶς, adv, sufficiently
²⁰ αἵρεσις, έσεως, ἡ, faction, heresy
²¹ ἐλέγχω aor act ind 3s, correct, reprove
²² ἐκκλησιαστικός, ή, όν, ecclesiastical
²³ κανών, όνος, ὁ, rule
²⁴ καθολικός, ή, όν, universal, general
²⁵ συναντάω aor act ptcp m.s.gen., meet
²⁶ ποτέ, adv, at some time
²⁷ Πολύκαρπος, ου, ὁ, Polycarp
²⁸ Μαρκίων, ωνος, ὁ, Marcion
²⁹ Μαρκιωνιστής, οῦ, ὁ, Marcionite
³⁰ Πολύκαρπος, ου, ὁ, Polycarp
³¹ Μαρκίων, ωνος, ὁ, Marcion
³² πρωτότοκος, ον, firstborn

Εἰρηναίου[1] συγγράμμασιν,[2] ὅτι ᾗ ἡμέρᾳ καὶ ὥρᾳ ἐν Σμύρνῃ[3] ἐμαρτύρησεν ὁ Πολύκαρπος,[4] ἤκουσεν φωνὴν ἐν τῇ Ῥωμαίων[5] πόλει ὑπάρχων ὁ Εἰρηναῖος,[6] ὡς σάλπιγγος[7] λεγούσης· Πολύκαρπος[8] ἐμαρτύρησεν. ἐκ τούτων οὖν, ὡς προλέλεκται,[9] τῶν τοῦ Εἰρηναίου[10] συγγραμμάτων[11] Γάϊος[12] μετεγράψατο,[13] ἐκ δὲ τῶν Γαΐου[14] ἀντιγράφων[15] Ἰσοκράτης[16] ἐν Κορίνθῳ.[17]

23:2 (22.3) Ἐγὼ δὲ πάλιν Πιόνιος[18] ἐκ τῶν Ἰσοκράτους[19] ἀντιγράφων[20] ἔγραψα, κατὰ ἀποκάλυψιν[21] τοῦ ἁγίου Πολυκάρπου[22] ζητήσας αὐτά, συναγαγὼν αὐτὰ ἤδη σχεδὸν[23] ἐκ τοῦ χρόνου κεκμηκότα,[24] ἵνα κἀμὲ συναγάγῃ ὁ κύριος Ἰησοῦς Χριστὸς μετὰ τῶν ἐκλεκτῶν[25] αὐτοῦ εἰς τὴν ἐπουράνιον[26] αὐτοῦ βασιλείαν· ᾧ ἡ δόξα σὺν τῷ πατρὶ καὶ τῷ υἱῷ καὶ τῷ ἁγίῳ πνεύματι εἰς τοὺς αἰῶνας τῶν αἰώνων, ἀμήν.

---

[1] Εἰρηναῖος, ου, ὁ, Irenaeus
[2] σύγγραμμα, ατος, τό, book, written work
[3] Σμύρνα, ης, ἡ, Smyrna
[4] Πολύκαρπος, ου, ὁ, Polycarp
[5] Ῥωμαῖος, α, ον, Roman
[6] Εἰρηναῖος, ου, ὁ, Irenaeus
[7] σάλπιγξ, ιγγος, ἡ, trumpet
[8] Πολύκαρπος, ου, ὁ, Polycarp
[9] προλέγω perf mid/pass ind 3s, tell beforehand
[10] Εἰρηναῖος, ου, ὁ, Irenaeus
[11] σύγγραμμα, ατος, τό, book, written work
[12] Γάϊος, ου, ὁ, Gaius
[13] μεταγράφω aor mid ind 3s, copy
[14] Γάϊος, ου, ὁ, Gaius
[15] ἀντίγραφον, ου, τό, copy
[16] Ἰσοκράτης, ους, ὁ, Isocrates
[17] Κόρινθος, ου, ἡ, Corinth
[18] Πιόνιος, ου, ὁ, Pionius
[19] Ἰσοκράτης, ους, ὁ, Isocrates
[20] ἀντίγραφον, ου, τό, copy
[21] ἀποκάλυψις, εως, ἡ, revelation
[22] Πολύκαρπος, ου, ὁ, Polycarp
[23] σχεδόν, adv, almost
[24] κάμνω perf act ptcp m.s.acc., worn out by age, fatigued
[25] ἐκλεκτός, ή, όν, elect, chosen
[26] ἐπουράνιος, ον, heavenly

Papias

APOSTOLIC FATHERS GREEK READER

Papias

An Introduction[*]

Papias, according to Eusebius, served as bishop in Hierapolis,[1] a city north of Laodicea and Colossae. He was associated with the Apostle John and was a contemporary of Polycarp (*ca.* pre-155–167?).[2] Irenaeus appeals to Papias as a proponent of Millenialism.[3] Papias's major work, entitled "Exposition of the Sayings of the Lord," serves as one of the earliest traditions that describes early Gospel composition.

Dating Papias

The minimal information about Papias prohibits definitive dates for his life. He is named among the early Christian leaders with Polycarp and Ignatius (*d.* 105–135).[4] Irenaeus calls him "a man of antiquity" (ἀρχαῖος ἀνήρ).[5] Papias is also a companion of Polycarp and a "hearer of John" the Apostle.[6] Papias's self-testimony indicates he prefers to hear from the living apostles as opposed to information in

---

[*] The current introduction to Papias is an edited version of: Shawn J. Wilhite, "Papias," in *The Lexham Bible Dictionary*, ed. John D. Barry and Lazarus Wentz (Bellingham, WA: Lexham Press, 2015).

[1] Eusebius *Hist.eccl.* III.36.1–2.

[2] Hubertus R. Drobner, *The Fathers of the Church: A Comprehensive Introduction*, trans. Siegried S. Schatzmann (Peabody, MA: Hendrickson, 2007), 45.

[3] Irenaeus *Adv. Haer.* V.33.4.

[4] Drobner, *Fathers of the Church*, 50.

[5] *Adv. Haer.* V.33.4; *Eccl. Hist.* III.39.1.

[6] *Adv. Haer.* V.33.4.

books.[1] These arguments support the arugment that Papias flourishes at least at the turn of the second century.[2]

Other arguments also demonstrate Papias living in a slightly later era. Older scholarship affirmed a late date for Papias's death (*ca.* 160).[3] Harnock[4] and Lightfoot[5] appeal to an anti-gnostic message found in his literature.[6] Papias fails to make clear who composed the Johannine material.[7] Even Eusebius further clarifies Papias's statments by suggesting that Papias mentions one John among the disciples and another John with Aristion (cf. the two tombs in Ephesus mentioned in *Eccl. Hist.* VII.25.17). The debate over two Johns and the Johannine material arose some years later.[8] Therefore, these arguments also support a later date for Papias's life.

One more consideration for dating Papias depends on how one understands his prologue.[9] Papias wrote his works after Mark, Matthew, 1 Peter, and 1 John. As a contemporary to Polycarp, Papias pre-dates Irenaeus (*d.* around 200).[10] Therefore, these chronological anchors help place Papias in an earlier historical context. Assuming the historical accuracy of his prologue, he is placed among the early disciples. "And if by chance someone who had been a follower of the elders should come my way, I inquired about the words of the elders—what

---

[1] Papias *Frag.* 3.4. Papias's enumeration depends upon: Michael W. Holmes, ed., *The Apostolic Fathers: Greek Texts and English Translations*, 3rd ed. (Grand Rapids: Baker Academic, 2007).

[2] Robert W. Yarbrough, "The Date of Papias: A Reassessment," *Journal of the Evangelical Theological Society* 26.2 (June 1983): 186.

[3] Yarbrough, "Date of Papias," 182.

[4] Adolf Harnack, *Geschichte der altchristlichen Literatur bis Eusebius*, 2nd ed. (Leipzig: J.C. Hinrichs, 1958).

[5] J. B. Lightfoot, *Essays on the Work Entitled Supernatural Religion* (London, UK: Macmillan, 1889).

[6] Yarbrough, "Date of Papias," 183.

[7] Papias *Frag.* 3.3–4.

[8] Yarbrough, "Date of Papias," 184.

[9] William R. Schoedel, *Polycarp, Martyrdom of Polycarp, Fragments of Papias*, Vol. 5, The Apostolic Fathers: A New Translation and Commentary (London, UK: Thomas Nelson & Sons, 1967), 136.

[10] Drobner, *Fathers of the Church*, 117.

Andrew or Peter said, or Philip or Thomas or James or John or Matthew or any other of the Lord's disciples, and whatever Aristion and the elder John, the Lord's disciples, were saying. For I did not think that information from books would profit me as much as information from a living and abiding voice."[1] Therefore, Richard Bauckham dates Papias's birth early (*ca.* 50).[2] Monte Shanks dates Papias at around the same time as Polycarp (*ca.* 70).[3]

Even less information is extant detailing Papias's death. According to an anonymous seventh-century work, *Chronicon Paschale*,[4] Papias is among those martyred in Pergamum. If true, Papias dies as a martyr in his early nineties. This martyrdom account, however, remains debated. The manuscript copyist may have mistakenly written Papias in lieu of Papylas.[5] If a copy error is present, then Papias may have died much earlier, as traditionally dated (*ca.* 130).[6]

Papias's Literature

Papias wrote five books entitled Λογίων Κυριακῶν Ἐξηγήσεως ("Exposition of the Sayings of the Lord").[7] However, they are no longer extant and we only have portions embedded in other early literature.[8] Eusebius's *Ecclesiastical History* contains the most amount of Papias's work.[9] Irenaeus is second in his *Against Heresies*.[10] Other sayings are found in the works of Apollinaris of Laodicea, Jerome,

---

[1] Papias *Frag.* 3.4.

[2] Richard Bauckham, *Jesus and the Eyewitnesses: The Gospels as Eyewitness Testimony* (Grand Rapids: Eerdmans, 2006), 18.

[3] Monte A. Shanks, *Papias and the New Testament* (Eugene, OR: Pickwick Publications, 2013), 65.

[4] PG 92.627.

[5] *Eccl. Hist.* IV.15.48.

[6] Shanks, *Papias*, 103–4; William R. Schoedel, "Papias," in *The Anchor Bible Dictionary*, Vol. 5 (New York: Double Day, 1992), 140.

[7] *Eccl. Hist.* III.39.1.

[8] Holmes, *Apostolic Fathers*, 722.

[9] *Eccl. Hist.* III.36.1–2; III.39.

[10] *Adv. Haer.* V.38.4.

Philip Sidetes, Andrew of Caesarea, Maximus the Confessor, and others.[1] The fragments, as we currently possess them, are intertwined with sayings and quotes from other literature. These fragments appear as either extended quotes of Papias, sayings about Papias, or a combination of both.[2]

It is impossible to determine the purpose of his letter given its fragmentary nature. The title, "Exposition of the Sayings of the Lord," may be an interpretation of either the words of Jesus or the words and deeds of Jesus. The meaning of the λογίων is difficult and has been taken in various ways.[3] The most probable meaning is "accounts of what Jesus said and did."[4] Schoedel summarizes how scholarship has viewed the purpose of Papias's book: to combat Gnosticism, Paulinism, the Gospel of John; or to establish the accuracy of the materials about Jesus though granting Matthew's superiority, Mark's lack of order, and John's gospel concern for historical order.[5]

Papias does, however, highlight the sources of his writings. "I will not hesitate to set down for you, along with my interpretations, everything I carefully learned then from the elders and carefully remembered, guaranteeing their truth."[6] The elders are later called John and Aristion.

---

[1] Clayton N. Jefford, *Reading the Apostolic Fathers: A Student's Introduction*, 2nd ed. (Grand Rapids: Baker Academic, 2012), 64–65.

[2] Jefford, *Reading the Apostolic Fathers*, 64.

[3] William R. Schoedel, "Papias," in *Principat 27.1*, ed. Wolfgang Haase, Aufstieg Und Niedergang Der Römischen Welt (Berlin, Germany: de Gruyter, 1993), 262–3; F. David Farnell, "The Synoptic Gospels in the Ancient Church: The Testimony to the Priority of Matthew's Gospel," *Master's Seminary Journal* 10.1 (Spring 1999): 56–69.

[4] Bauckham, *Jesus and the Eyewitnesses*, 12n2.

[5] Schoedel, "Papias," in *Principat 27.1*, 246–47.

[6] Papias *Frag.* 3.3.

Relevance to New Testament Studies and Christian Theology

Papias is more known for his comments on Matthew, Peter's relationship to Mark, and early views on Chiliasm. The following briefly highlights portions of Papias's comments and his relevance to biblical studies.

Papias provides an early tradition on Gospel composition. The Gospel of Mark has a Petrine tradition. Mark interprets all that he remembers from the apostle Peter. "Mark, having become Peter's interpreter, wrote down accurately everything he remembered, though not in order, of the things either said or done by Christ. For he neither heard the Lord nor followed him, but afterward, as I said, followed Peter, who adapted his teachings as needed but had no intention of giving an ordered account of the Lord's sayings. Consequently Mark did nothing wrong in writing down some things as he remembered them, for he made it his one concern not to omit anything that he heard or to make any false statement in them."[1] According to this quote, Mark is the interpreter and redactor of Peter's eyewitness accounts. Papias also claims Mark is not written in historical order.[2]

According to Papias, the Gospel of Matthew has a Semitic background. "So Matthew composed the oracles in the Hebrew language and each person interpreted them as best he could."[3] Though no extant Aramaic or Hebrew MS exists of the Gospel of Matthew, Papias says Matthew originally composed the oracles Ἑβραΐδι διαλέκτῳ ("to/in the Hebrew dialect"). This phrase is interpreted variously within scholarship too.[4] Either Matthew composed it *to the Hebrew dialect*, saying something about a Semitic audience, or *in the Hebrew dialect*, saying something about language of composition or style.[5] Papias's

---

[1] Papias *Frag.* 3.15.

[2] Richard Bauckham, *The Testimony of the Beloved Disciple: Narrative, History, and Theology in the Gospel of John* (Grand Rapids, MI: Baker Academic, 2007), 51–58; Bauckham, *Jesus and the Eyewitnesses*, 202–39.

[3] Papias *Frag.* 3.16.

[4] Schoedel, "Papias," in *Principat 27.1*, 262.

[5] Bauckham, *Jesus and the Eyewitnesses*, 222–24.

comments on Matthew and Mark have influenced some discussions related to the Synoptic Problem.[1]

Papias also holds to Millinarianism, or Chiliasm, and gives early testimony to a particular eschatological position. Eusebius, in response, critiques his intelligence for holding such views. "Among other things he says that after the resurrection of the dead there will be a period of a thousand years when the kingdom of Christ will be set up in material form on this earth. These ideas, I suppose, he though through a misunderstanding of the apostolic accounts, not realizing that the things recorded in figurative language were spoken by them mystically. For he certainly appears to be a man of very little intelligence, as one may say judging from his own words."[2] Moreover, Irenaeus and others expressed similar ideas.[3]

Papias's comments may have two different John's involved in the composition of the Johannine literature.[4] Philip Sidetes says, "some think that this John (i.e. John the Elder) is the author of the two short Catholic Epistles that circulate under the name John, because the people of the earliest period accept only the first epistle."[5] Jerome provides a similar observation.[6]

Another influence of Papias's literature concerns the *Pericope Adulterate* (John 7:53–8:11). Eusebius recalls Papias telling the account "about a woman accused of many sins before the Lord, which the *Gospel according to the Hebrews* contains."[7] This comment assists early traditions and text-critical observations for this form unit. Later traditions credit Papias for inserting this pericope into the

---

[1] Schoedel, "Papias," in *Principat 27.1*, 265–67.

[2] Papias *Frag.* 3.12–13.

[3] *Eccl. His.* III.39.13; *Adv. Haer.* V.33.4.

[4] Papias *Frag.* 3.3–4.

[5] Papias *Frag.* 5.3.

[6] Papias *Frag.* 7.5–7; In *Beloved Disciple*, Bauckham provides a definitive work interacting with the historical tradition of Papias and John.

[7] Papias *Frag.* 3.17.

Gospel of John.[1] Moreover, Codex Vaticanus Alexandrinus (9th Cent) credits Papias as John's amanuensis for his Gospel.[2]

Papias also contributes to the history of interpretation for Acts 1:18. Apollinaris of Laodicaea (4th century) records a large portion from the *Expositions of the Sayings of the Lord*. "Judas was a terrible, walking example of ungodliness in this world, his flesh so bloated that he was not able to pass through a place where a wagon passes easily, not even his bloated head by itself. For his eyelids, they say, were so swollen that he could not see the light at all, and his eyes could not be seen, even by a doctor using an optical instrument, so far had they sunk below the outer surface. His genitals appeared more loathsome and larger than anyone else's, and when he relieved himself there passed through it pus and worms from every part of his body, much to his shame. After much agony and punishment, they say, he finally died in his own place, and because of the stench the area is deserted and uninhabitable even now; in fact, to this day one cannot pass that place without holding one's nose, so great was the discharge from his body, and so far did it spread over the ground."[3] So rather than hanging and immediately dying, Papias provides an early interpretation and testimony that Judas lived and miserably died at a later time.

Shawn J. Wilhite

---

[1] Papias *Frag.* 26.
[2] Papias *Frag.* 19.
[3] Papias *Frag.* 18.4–7.

Fragments of Papias

NOTES BY MATTHEW MCMAINS

1:1 Ἰωάννην τὸν θεολόγον,[1] καὶ ἀπόστολον Εἰρηναῖος[2] καὶ ἄλλοι ἱστοροῦσι[3] παραμεῖναι[4] τῷ βίῳ[5] ἕως τῶν χρόνων Τραϊανοῦ.[6] μεθ᾽ ὃν Παπίας[7] Ἱεραπολίτης[8] καὶ Πολύκαρπος[9] Σμύρνης[10] ἐπίσκοπος[11] ἀκουσταὶ[12] αὐτοῦ ἐγνωρίζοντο.[13]

2:1 Διέπρεπέ[14] γε[15] μὴν κατὰ τούτους ἐπὶ τῆς Ἀσίας[16] τῶν ἀποστόλων ὁμιλητὴς[17] Πολύκαρπος,[18] τῆς κατὰ Σμύρναν[19] ἐκκλησίας πρὸς τῶν αὐτοπτῶν[20] καὶ ὑπηρετῶν[21] τοῦ Κυρίου τὴν ἐπισκοπὴν[22] ἐγκεχειρισμένος.[23] καθ᾽ ὃν ἐγνωρίζετο[24] Παπίας[25] τῆς ἐν Ἱεραπόλει[26] παροικίας[27] καὶ αὐτὸς ἐπίσκοπος.[28]

---

[1] θεολόγος, ου, ὁ, theologian, herald
[2] Εἰρηναῖος, ου, ὁ, Irenaeus
[3] ἱστορέω pres act ind 3p, record
[4] παραμένω aor act inf, remain
[5] βίος, ου, ὁ, life
[6] Τραϊανός, ου, ὁ, Trajan
[7] Παπίας, α or ου, ὁ, Papias
[8] Ἱεραπολίτης, ου, ὁ, Hierapolite; a citizen of Hierapolis
[9] Πολύκαρπος, ου, ὁ, Polycarp
[10] Σμύρνα, ης, ἡ, Smyrna
[11] ἐπίσκοπος, ου, ὁ, bishop
[12] ἀκουστής, οῦ, ὁ, hearer
[13] γνωρίζω imp mid/pass ind 3p, make known
[14] διαπρέπω imp act ind 3s, flourish
[15] γέ, part, indeed
[16] Ἀσία, ας, ἡ, Asia
[17] ὁμιλητής, οῦ, ὁ, disciple
[18] Πολύκαρπος, ου, ὁ, Polycarp
[19] Σμύρνα, ης, ἡ, Smyrna
[20] αὐτόπτης, ου, ὁ, eyewitness
[21] ὑπηρέτης, ου, ὁ, minister
[22] ἐπίσκοπος, ου, ὁ, bishop
[23] ἐγχειρίζω perf mid/pass ptcp m.s.nom., entrust
[24] γνωρίζω imp mid/pass ind 3p, make known
[25] Παπίας, α or ου, ὁ, Papias
[26] Ἱεράπολις, εως, ἡ, Hierapolis
[27] παροικία, ας, ἡ, district
[28] ἐπίσκοπος, ου, ὁ, bishop

3:1 Τοῦ δὲ Παπία¹ συγγράμματα² πέντε τὸν ἀριθμὸν³ φέρεται, ἃ καὶ ἐπιγέγραπται⁴ λογίων⁵ κυριακῶν⁶ ἐξηγήσεως⁷ τούτων καὶ Εἰρηναῖος⁸ ὡς μόνων αὐτῷ γραφέντων μνημονεύει,⁹ ὧδε πως¹⁰ λέγων· ταῦτα δὲ καὶ Παπίας¹¹ ὁ Ἰωάννου μὲν ἀκουστής¹² Πολυκάρπου¹³ δὲ ἑταῖρος¹⁴ γεγονώς, ἀρχαῖος¹⁵ ἀνήρ, ἐγγράφως¹⁶ ἐπιμαρτυρεῖ¹⁷ ἐν τῇ τετάρτῃ¹⁸ τῶν ἑαυτοῦ βιβλίων· ἔστιν γὰρ αὐτῷ πέντε βιβλία συντεταγμένα.¹⁹ **2** Καὶ ὁ μὲν Εἰρηναῖος²⁰ ταῦτα. Αὐτός γε²¹ μὴν ὁ Παπίας²² κατὰ τὸ προοίμιον²³ τῶν αὐτοῦ λόγων ἀκροατὴν²⁴ μὲν καὶ αὐτόπτην²⁵ οὐδαμῶς²⁶ ἑαυτὸν γενέσθαι τῶν ἱερῶν²⁷ ἀποστόλων ἐμφαίνει,²⁸ παρειληφέναι δὲ τὰ τῆς πίστεως παρὰ τῶν ἐκείνοις γνωρίμων²⁹ διδάσκει δι' ὧν φησιν λέξεων.³⁰

3:3 Οὐκ ὀκνήσω³¹ δέ σοι καὶ ὅσα ποτὲ³² παρὰ τῶν πρεσβυτέρων καλῶς ἔμαθον³³ καὶ καλῶς ἐμνημόνευσα,³⁴ συγκατατάξαι³⁵ ταῖς

---

¹ Παπίας, α or ου, ὁ, Papias
² σύγγραμμα, ατος, τό, book
³ ἀριθμός, οῦ, ὁ, number
⁴ ἐπιγράφω perf mid/pass ind 3s, write
⁵ λόγιον, ου, τό, saying
⁶ κυριακός, ή, όν, belonging to the Lord
⁷ ἐξήγησις, εως, ἡ, narrative
⁸ Εἰρηναῖος, ου, ὁ, Irenaeus
⁹ μνημονεύω pres act ind 3s, remember, mention
¹⁰ πως, adv, manner, in some way
¹¹ Παπίας, α or ου, ὁ, Papias
¹² ἀκουστής, οῦ, ὁ, hearer
¹³ Πολύκαρπος, ου, ὁ, Polycarp
¹⁴ ἑταῖρος, ου, ὁ, companion
¹⁵ ἀρχαῖος, αία, αῖον, ancient
¹⁶ ἐγγράφως, adv, in writing
¹⁷ ἐπιμαρτυρέω pres act ind 3s, bear witness
¹⁸ τέταρτος, η, ον, fourth
¹⁹ συντάσσω perf mid/pass ptcp n.p.nom., appoint, arrange, compose
²⁰ Εἰρηναῖος, ου, ὁ, Irenaeus
²¹ γέ, part, indeed
²² Παπίας, α or ου, ὁ, Papias
²³ προοίμιον, ου, τό, preface
²⁴ ἀκροατής, οῦ, ὁ, hearer
²⁵ αὐτόπτης, ου, ὁ, eyewitness
²⁶ οὐδαμῶς, adv, by no means
²⁷ ἱερός, ά, όν, holy
²⁸ ἐμφαίνω pres act ind 3s, exhibit
²⁹ γνώριμος, ον, acquainted
³⁰ λέξις, εως, ἡ, speech
³¹ ὀκνέω fut act ind 1s, hesitate
³² ποτέ, conj, at some time
³³ μανθάνω aor act ind 1s, learn
³⁴ μνημονεύω aor act ind 1s, remember
³⁵ συγκατατάσσω aor act inf, set forth things along with

ἑρμηνείαις,[1] διαβεβαιούμενος[2] ὑπὲρ αὐτῶν ἀλήθειαν. οὐ γὰρ τοῖς τὰ πολλὰ λέγουσιν ἔχαιρον ὥσπερ οἱ πολλοί, ἀλλὰ τοῖς τἀληθῆ[3] διδάσκουσιν, οὐδὲ τοῖς τὰς ἀλλοτρίας[4] ἐντολὰς μνημονεύουσιν,[5] ἀλλὰ τοῖς τὰς παρὰ τοῦ Κυρίου τῇ πίστει δεδομένας καὶ ἀπ' αὐτῆς παραγινομένας τῆς ἀληθείας. **4** Εἰ δέ που[6] καὶ παρηκολουθηκώς[7] τις τοῖς πρεσβυτέροις ἔλθοι, τοὺς τῶν πρεσβυτέρων ἀνέκρινον[8] λόγους· τί Ἀνδρέας[9] ἢ τί Πέτρος εἶπεν ἢ τί Φίλιππος ἢ τί Θωμᾶς[10] ἢ Ἰάκωβος ἢ τί Ἰωάννης ἢ Ματθαῖος[11] ἢ τις ἕτερος τῶν τοῦ Κυρίου μαθητῶν, ἅ τε Ἀριστίων[12] καὶ ὁ πρεσβύτερος Ἰωάννης, οἱ τοῦ Κυρίου μαθηταί, λέγουσιν. οὐ γὰρ τὰ ἐκ τῶν βιβλίων τοσοῦτόν[13] με ὠφελεῖν[14] ὑπελάμβανον,[15] ὅσον τὰ παρὰ ζώσης φωνῆς καὶ μενούσης.

3:5 Ἔνθα[16] καὶ ἐπιστῆσαι[17] ἄξιον δὶς[18] καταριθμοῦντι[19] αὐτῷ τὸ Ἰωάννου ὄνομα, ὧν τὸν μὲν πρότερον[20] Πέτρῳ καὶ Ἰακώβῳ καὶ Ματθαίῳ[21] καὶ τοῖς λοιποῖς ἀποστόλοις συγκαταλέγει,[22] σαφῶς[23] δηλῶν[24] τὸν εὐαγγελιστήν,[25] τὸν δ' ἕτερον Ἰωάννην διαστείλας[26] τὸν λόγον ἑτέροις παρὰ τὸν τῶν ἀποστόλων

---

[1] ἑρμηνεία, ας, ἡ, interpretation
[2] διαβεβαιόω pres mid/pass ptcp m.s.nom., 1s, confirm
[3] ἀληθής, ές, true
[4] ἀλλότριος, ία, ον, belonging to another
[5] μνημονεύω pres act ptcp m.p.dat., remember
[6] πού, adv, somewhere
[7] παρακολουθέω perf act ptcp m.s.nom., follow
[8] ἀνακρίνω imp act ind 1s, examine
[9] Ἀνδρέας, ου, ὁ, Andrew
[10] Θωμᾶς, ᾶ, ὁ, Thomas
[11] Ματθαῖος, ου, ὁ, Matthew
[12] Ἀριστίων, ωνος, ὁ, Aristion
[13] τοσοῦτος, αύτη, οῦτον, so much

[14] ὠφελέω imp act ind 1s, help, aid, profit
[15] ὑπολαμβάνω pres act inf, think
[16] ἔνθα, adv, there
[17] ἐφίστημι aor act inf, set
[18] δίς, adv, twice
[19] καταριθμέω pres act ptcp m.s.dat., enumerate
[20] πρότερος, adv, formerly
[21] Ματθαῖος, ου, ὁ, Matthew
[22] συγκαταλέγω pres act ind 3s, lay down with, mention
[23] σαφῶς, adv, clearly
[24] δηλόω pres act ptcp m.s.nom., make clear, indicate
[25] εὐαγγελιστής, οῦ, ὁ, evangelist
[26] διαστέλλω aor act ptcp m.s.nom., command

ἀριθμὸν[1] κατατάσσει,[2] προτάξας[3] αὐτοῦ τὸν Ἀριστίωνα,[4] **6** σαφῶς[5] τε αὐτὸν πρεσβύτερον ὀνομάζει·[6] ὡς καὶ διὰ τούτων ἀποδείκνυσθαι[7] τὴν ἱστορίαν[8] ἀληθῆ[9] τῶν δύο κατὰ τὴν Ἀσίαν[10] ὁμωνυμίᾳ[11] κεχρῆσθαι[12] εἰρηκότων, δύο τε ἐν Ἐφέσῳ[13] γενέσθαι μνήματα[14] καὶ ἑκάτερον[15] Ἰωάννου ἔτι νῦν λέγεσθαι. Οἷς καὶ ἀναγκαῖον[16] προσέχειν[17] τὸν νοῦν·[18] εἰκὸς[19] γὰρ τὸν δεύτερον, εἰ μή τις ἐθέλοι τὸν πρῶτον, τὴν ἐπ' ὀνόματος φερομένην Ἰωάννου ἀποκάλυψιν[20] ἑωρακέναι. **7** Καὶ ὁ νῦν δὲ ἡμῖν δηλούμενος[21] Παπίας[22] τοὺς μὲν τῶν ἀποστόλων λόγους παρὰ τῶν αὐτοῖς παρηκολουθηκότων[23] ὁμολογεῖ[24] παρειληφέναι, Ἀριστίωνος[25] δὲ καὶ τοῦ πρεσβυτέρου Ἰωάννου αὐτήκοον[26] ἑαυτόν φησι γενέσθαι. Ὀνομαστὶ[27] γοῦν[28] πολλάκις[29] αὐτῶν μνημονεύσας,[30] ἐν τοῖς αὐτοῦ συγγράμμασι[31] τίθησιν αὐτῶν καὶ παραδόσεις.[32] Καὶ ταῦτα δ' ἡμῖν οὐκ εἰς τὸ ἄχρηστον[33] εἰρήσθω.

---

[1] ἀριθμός, οῦ, ὁ, number
[2] κατατάσσω pres act ind 3s, appoint
[3] προτάσσω aor act ptcp, m.s.nom., ordain, put before
[4] Ἀριστίων, ωνος, ὁ, Aristion
[5] σαφῶς, adv, clearly
[6] ὀνομάζω pres act ind 3s, name
[7] ἀποδείκνυμι pres mid/pass inf, show, confirm
[8] ἱστορία, ας, ἡ, account, story
[9] ἀληθής, ές, true
[10] Ἀσία, ας, ἡ, Asia
[11] ὁμωνυμία, ας, ἡ, having the same name
[12] χράομαι perf mid/pass inf, use
[13] Ἔφεσος, ου, ἡ, Ephesus
[14] μνῆμα, ατος, τό, grave, tomb
[15] ἑκάτερος, α, ον, each, both
[16] ἀναγκαῖος, α, ον, necessary
[17] προσέχω pres act inf, pay attention, notice
[18] νοῦς, ός, ὁ, mind, intellect
[19] εἰκός, ότος, τό, probable, reasonable
[20] ἀποκάλυψις, εως, ἡ, revelation
[21] δηλόω pres mid/pass ptcp m.s.nom., make known, speak
[22] Παπίας, ου, ὁ, Papias
[23] παρακολουθέω perf act ptcp m.p.gen., follow
[24] ὁμολογέω pres act ind 3s, promise, acknowledge
[25] Ἀριστίων, ωνος, ὁ, Aristion
[26] αὐτήκοος, ον, hearer
[27] ὀνομαστί, adv, by name
[28] γοῦν, part, hence, in any event
[29] πολλάκις, adv, frequently
[30] μνημονεύω aor act ptcp m.s.nom., remember, mention
[31] σύγγραμμα, ατος, τό, writing, book
[32] παράδοσις, εως, ἡ, tradition
[33] ἄχρηστος, ον, useless

3:8 Ἄξιον δὲ ταῖς ἀποδοθείσαις τοῦ Παπία[1] φωναῖς προσάψαι[2] λέξεις[3] ἑτέρας αὐτοῦ, δι' ὧν παράδοξά[4] τινα ἱστορεῖ[5] καὶ ἄλλα, ὡς ἂν ἐκ παραδόσεως[6] εἰς αὐτὸν ἐλθόντα. **9** Τὸ μὲν οὖν κατὰ τὴν Ἱεράπολιν[7] Φίλιππον τὸν ἀπόστολον ἅμα[8] ταῖς θυγατράσι[9] διατρῖψαι,[10] διὰ τῶν πρόσθεν[11] δεδήλωται,[12] ὡς δὲ κατὰ τοὺς αὐτοὺς ὁ Παπίας[13] γενόμενος διήγησιν[14] παρειληφέναι θαυμασίαν[15] ὑπὸ τῶν τοῦ Φιλίππου θυγατέρων[16] μνημονεύει,[17] τὰ νῦν σημειωτέον.[18] Νεκροῦ γὰρ ἀνάστασιν κατ' αὐτὸν γεγονυῖαν ἱστορεῖ,[19] καὶ αὖ[20] πάλιν ἕτερον παράδοξον[21] περὶ Ἰοῦστον[22] τὸν ἐπικληθέντα Βαρσαββᾶν[23] γεγονός, ὡς δηλητήριον[24] φάρμακον[25] ἐμπιόντος[26] καὶ μηδὲν ἀηδὲς[27] διὰ τὴν τοῦ Κυρίου χάριν ὑπομείναντος.[28] **10** Τοῦτον δὲ τὸν Ἰοῦστον[29] μετὰ τὴν τοῦ σωτῆρος[30] ἀνάληψιν[31] τοὺς ἱεροὺς[32] ἀποστόλους μετὰ Ματθία[33] στῆσαί τε καὶ ἐπεύξασθαι[34] ἀντὶ[35] τοῦ

---

[1] Παπίας, α or ου, ὁ, Papias
[2] προσάπτω aor act inf, add
[3] λέξις, εως, ἡ, speech; a word
[4] παράδοξος, ον, strange, remarkable
[5] ἱστορέω pres act ind 3s, record
[6] παράδοσις, εως, ἡ, tradition
[7] Ἱεράπολις, εως, ἡ, Hierapolis
[8] ἅμα, impr prep, together, at the same time
[9] θυγάτηρ, τρός, ἡ, daughter
[10] διατρίβω aor act inf, stay in the same place, reside
[11] πρόσθεν, adv, earlier, former
[12] δηλόω perf mid/pass ind 3s, reveal, make clear
[13] Παπίας, α or ου, ὁ, Papias
[14] διήγησις, εως, ἡ, narrative, account
[15] θαυμάσιος, α, ον, amazing
[16] θυγάτηρ, τρός, ἡ, daughter
[17] μνημονεύω pres act ind 3s, remember, mention

[18] σημειωτέος, α, ον, one must point out
[19] ἱστορέω pres act ind 3s, record
[20] αὖ, adv, anew, afresh
[21] παράδοξος, ον, strange, remarkable
[22] Ἰοῦστος, ου, ὁ, Justus
[23] Βαρσαββᾶς, ᾶ, ὁ, Barsabbas
[24] δηλητήριος, α, ον, lethal
[25] φάρμακον, ου, τό, poison
[26] ἐμπίνω aor act ptcp m.s.gen., drink
[27] ἀηδής, ές, unpleasant
[28] ὑπομένω aor act ptcp m.s.gen., endure
[29] Ἰοῦστος, ου, ὁ, Justus
[30] σωτήρ, ῆρος, ὁ, Savior
[31] ἀνάλημψις, εως, ἡ, revelation, Apocalypse
[32] ἱερός, ά, όν, holy
[33] Ματθίας, ου, ὁ, Matthias
[34] ἐπεύχομαι aor mid inf, pray
[35] ἀντί, prep, in place of

προδότου[1] Ἰούδα[2] ἐπὶ τὸν κλῆρον[3] τῆς ἀναπληρώσεως[4] τοῦ αὐτῶν ἀριθμοῦ,[5] ἡ τῶν πράξεων[6] ὧδε πως[7] ἱστορεῖ[8] γραφή· Καὶ ἔστησαν δύο, Ἰωσὴφ τὸν καλούμενον Βαρσαββᾶν,[9] ὃς ἐπεκλήθη Ἰοῦστος,[10] καὶ Ματθίαν·[11] καὶ προσευξάμενοι εἶπαν. **11** Καὶ ἄλλα δὲ ὁ αὐτὸς ὡσὰν[12] ἐκ παραδόσεως[13] ἀγράφου[14] εἰς αὐτὸν ἥκοντα[15] παρατέθειται,[16] ξένας[17] τέ τινας παραβολὰς τοῦ Σωτῆρος[18] καὶ διδασκαλίας[19] αὐτοῦ, καὶ τινα ἄλλα μυθικώτερα.[20] **12** Ἐν οἷς καὶ χιλιάδα[21] τινά φησιν ἐτῶν ἔσεσθαι μετὰ τὴν ἐκ νεκρῶν ἀνάστασιν, σωματικῶς[22] τῆς Χριστοῦ βασιλείας ἐπὶ ταυτησὶ[23] τῆς γῆς ὑποστησομένης.[24] Ἃ καὶ ἡγοῦμαι[25] τὰς ἀποστολικὰς[26] παρεκδεξάμενον[27] διηγήσεις[28] ὑπολαβεῖν,[29] τὰ ἐν ὑποδείγμασι[30] πρὸς αὐτῶν μυστικῶς[31] εἰρημένα μὴ συνεωρακότα.[32]

13 Σφόδρα[33] γάρ τοι[34] σμικρὸς ὢν τὸν νοῦν,[35] ὡς ἂν ἐκ τῶν αὐτοῦ

---

[1] προδότης, ου, ὁ, traitor

[2] Ἰούδα, Judas

[3] κλῆρος, ου, ὁ, lot

[4] ἀναπλήρωσις, εως, ἡ, fill up

[5] ἀριθμός, οῦ, ὁ, number

[6] πρᾶξις, εως, ἡ, action, undertaking, deed

[7] πως, part, in some way

[8] ἱστορέω pres act ind 3s, record

[9] Βαρσαβᾶς, ᾶ, ὁ, Barsabbas

[10] Ἰοῦστος, ου, ὁ, Justus

[11] Ματθίας, ου, ὁ, Matthias

[12] ὡσάν, conj, as if

[13] παράδοσις, εως, ἡ, tradition

[14] ἄγραφος, α, ον, unwritten

[15] ἥκω pres act ptcp m.s.acc., to have come

[16] παρατίθημι perf mid/pass ind 3s, set before

[17] ξένος, η, ον, unfamiliar, strange

[18] σωτήρ, ῆρος, ὁ, savior

[19] διδασκαλία, ας, ἡ, teaching

[20] μυθικός, ή, όν, mythical

[21] χιλιάς, άδος, ἡ, a thousand

[22] σωματικῶς, adv, bodily, materially

[23] οὑτοσί, adv, here

[24] ὑφίστημι fut mid ptcp f.s.gen., set up

[25] ἡγέομαι pres mid/pass ind 3s, think, suppose

[26] ἀποστολικός, ή, όν, apostolic

[27] παρεκδέχομαι aor mid ptcp, m.s.nom., misinterpret

[28] διήγησις, εως, ἡ, account

[29] ὑπολαμβάνω aor act inf, take up

[30] ὑπόδειγμα, ατος, τό, symbol

[31] μυστικῶς, adv, mystically

[32] συνοράω perf act ptcp n.p.acc., perceive, realize

[33] σφόδρα, adv, very

[34] τοί, part, surely

[35] νοῦς, ός, ὁ, intellect

λόγων τεκμηράμενον[1] εἰπεῖν, φαίνεται· πλὴν καὶ τοῖς μετ' αὐτὸν πλείστοις ὅσοις τῶν ἐκκλησιαστικῶν[2] τῆς ὁμοίας αὐτῷ δόξης παραίτιος[3] γέγονεν, τὴν ἀρχαιότητα[4] τἀνδρὸς προβεβλημένοις,[5] ὥσπερ οὖν Εἰρηναίῳ,[6] καὶ εἴ τις ἄλλος τὰ ὅμοια φρονῶν[7] ἀναπέφηνεν.[8] **14** Καὶ ἄλλας δὲ τῇ ἑαυτοῦ γραφῇ παραδίδωσιν Ἀριστίωνος[9] τοῦ πρόσθεν[10] δεδηλωμένου[11] τῶν τοῦ Κυρίου λόγων διηγήσεις[12] καὶ τοῦ πρεσβυτέρου Ἰωάννου παραδόσεις,[13] ἐφ' ἃς τοὺς φιλομαθεῖς[14] ἀναπέμψαντες,[15] ἀναγκαίως[16] νῦν προσθήσομεν[17] ταῖς προεκτεθείσαις[18] αὐτοῦ φωναῖς παράδοσιν,[19] ἣν περὶ Μάρκου[20] τοῦ τὸ εὐαγγέλιον γεγραφότος ἐκτέθειται[21] διὰ τούτων·

3:15 Καὶ τοῦτο ὁ πρεσβύτερος ἔλεγε· Μάρκος[22] μὲν ἑρμηνευτὴς[23] Πέτρου γενόμενος, ὅσα ἐμνημόνευσεν,[24] ἀκριβῶς[25] ἔγραψεν, οὐ μέντοι[26] τάξει,[27] τὰ ὑπὸ τοῦ Χριστοῦ ἢ λεχθέντα ἢ πραχθέντα. οὔτε γὰρ ἤκουσε τοῦ Κυρίου, οὔτε παρηκολού-

---

[1] τεκμαίρομαι aor mid ptcp m.s.acc., judge
[2] ἐκκλησιαστικός, ή, όν, ecclesiastical
[3] παραίτιος, ον, share
[4] ἀρχαιότης, ητος, ἡ, antiquity, early period
[5] προβάλλω perf mid/pass ptcp m.p.dat., put forward
[6] Εἰρηναῖος, ου, ὁ, Irenaeus
[7] φρονέω pres act ptcp m.s.nom., hold an opinion
[8] ἀναφαίνω perf act ind 3s, appear
[9] Ἀριστίων, ωνος, ὁ, Aristion
[10] πρόσθεν, adv, formerly
[11] δηλόω perf mid/pass ptcp m.s.gen., reveal, mention
[12] διήγησις, εως, ἡ, narrative, account
[13] παράδοσις, εως, ἡ, tradition
[14] φιλομαθής, ές, fond of learning, eager after knowledge
[15] ἀναπέμπω aor act ptcp m.p.nom., send, refer
[16] ἀναγκαίως, adv, necessarily
[17] προστίθημι fut act ind 1p, add
[18] προεκτίθημι aor pass ptcp f.p.dat., set forth, expound before
[19] παράδοσις, εως, ἡ, tradition
[20] Μάρκος, ου, ὁ, Mark
[21] ἐκτίθημι perf mid/pass ind 3s, explain
[22] Μάρκος, ου, ὁ, Mark
[23] ἑρμηνευτής, οῦ, ὁ, interpreter
[24] μνημονεύω aor act ind 3s, remember
[25] ἀκριβῶς, adv, accurately
[26] μέντοι, part, though
[27] τάξις, εως, ἡ, sequence, order

θησεν[1] αὐτῷ, ὕστερον[2] δέ, ὡς ἔφην, Πέτρῳ, ὃς πρὸς τὰς χρείας ἐποιεῖτο τὰς διδασκαλίας,[3] ἀλλ' οὐχ ὥσπερ σύνταξιν[4] τῶν κυριακῶν[5] ποιούμενος λογίων,[6] ὥστε οὐδὲν ἥμαρτε Μάρκος,[7] οὕτως ἔνια[8] γράψας ὡς ἀπεμνημόνευσεν.[9] ἑνὸς γὰρ ἐποιήσατο πρόνοιαν,[10] τοῦ μηδὲν ὧν ἤκουσε παραλιπεῖν[11] ἢ ψεύσασθαί[12] τι ἐν αὐτοῖς. Ταῦτα μὲν οὖν ἱστόρηται[13] τῷ Παπίᾳ[14] περὶ τοῦ Μάρκου.[15] **16** Περὶ δὲ τοῦ Ματθαίου[16] ταῦτ' εἴρηται· Ματθαῖος[17] μὲν οὖν Ἑβραΐδι[18] διαλέκτῳ[19] τὰ λόγια[20] συνετάξατο,[21] ἑρμήνευσε[22] δ' αὐτὰ ὡς ἦν δυνατὸς ἕκαστος.

3:17 Κέχρηται[23] δ' αὐτὸς μαρτυρίαις ἀπὸ τῆς Ἰωάννου προτέρας[24] ἐπιστολῆς καὶ ἀπὸ τῆς Πέτρου ὁμοίως. ἐκτέθειται[25] δὲ καὶ ἄλλην ἱστορίαν[26] περὶ γυναικὸς ἐπὶ πολλαῖς ἁμαρτίαις διαβληθείσης[27] ἐπὶ τοῦ Κυρίου, ἣν τὸ κατ' Ἑβραίους[28]

---

[1] παρακολουθέω aor act ind 3s, follow
[2] ὕστερος, α, ον, later, thereafter
[3] διδασκαλία, ας, ἡ, teaching
[4] σύνταξις, εως, ἡ, organized account
[5] κυριακός, ή, όν, belonging to the Lord
[6] λόγιον, ου, τό, saying
[7] Μᾶρκος, ου, ὁ, Mark
[8] ἔνιοι, αι, α, some, several
[9] ἀπομνημονεύω aor act ind 3s, remember
[10] πρόνοια, ας, ἡ, forethought, concern
[11] παραλείπω aor act inf, omit
[12] ψεύδομαι aor mid inf, tell a lie
[13] ἱστορέω perf mid/pass ind 3s, record

[14] Παπίας, ου, ὁ, Papias
[15] Μᾶρκος, ου, ὁ, Mark
[16] Ματθίας, ου, ὁ, Matthias
[17] Ματθίας, ου, ὁ, Matthias
[18] Ἑβραΐς, ΐδος, ἡ, Hebrew
[19] διάλεκτος, ου, ἡ, language
[20] λόγιον, ου, τό, saying
[21] συντάσσω aor mid ind 3s, arrange, compose
[22] ἑρμηνεύω aor act ind 3s, interpret
[23] χράομαι perf mid/pass ind 3s, make use of, employ
[24] πρότερος, α, ον, earlier, former
[25] ἐκτίθημι perf mid/pass ind 3s, explain, relate
[26] ἱστορία, ας, ἡ, account
[27] διαβάλλω aor pass ptcp f.s.gen., accuse
[28] Ἑβραῖος, ου, ὁ, Hebrew

εὐαγγέλιον περιέχει.[1] Καὶ ταῦτα δ' ἡμῖν ἀναγκαίως[2] πρὸς τοῖς ἐκτεθεῖσιν[3] ἐπιτετηρήσθω.[4]

4:1 Καὶ ἐπορεύθησαν ἕκαστος εἰς τὸν οἶκον αὐτοῦ, Ἰησοῦς δὲ ἐπορεύθη εἰς τὸ Ὄρος τῶν Ἐλαιῶν.[5] ὄρθρου[6] δὲ πάλιν παρεγένετο εἰς τὸ ἱερόν, καὶ πᾶς ὁ λαὸς ἤρχετο πρὸς αὐτόν, καὶ καθίσας ἐδίδασκεν. ἄγουσιν δὲ οἱ γραμματεῖς καὶ οἱ Φαρισαῖοι γυναῖκα ἐπὶ μοιχείᾳ[7] κατειλημμένην,[8] καὶ στήσαντες αὐτὴν ἐν μέσῳ λέγουσιν αὐτῷ Διδάσκαλε, αὕτη ἡ γυνὴ κατείληπται[9] ἐπ' αὐτοφώρῳ[10] μοιχευομένη.[11] ἐν δὲ τῷ νόμῳ ἡμῖν Μωυσῆς ἐνετείλατο[12] τὰς τοιαύτας λιθάζειν·[13] σὺ οὖν τί λέγεις; τοῦτο δὲ ἔλεγον πειράζοντες αὐτόν, ἵνα ἔχωσιν κατηγορεῖν[14] αὐτοῦ. ὁ δὲ Ἰησοῦς κάτω[15] κύψας[16] τῷ δακτύλῳ[17] κατέγραφεν[18] εἰς τὴν γῆν. ὡς δὲ ἐπέμενον[19] ἐρωτῶντες αὐτόν, ἀνέκυψεν[20] καὶ εἶπεν αὐτοῖς Ὁ ἀναμάρτητος[21] ὑμῶν πρῶτος ἐπ' αὐτὴν βαλέτω λίθον· καὶ πάλιν κατακύψας[22] ἔγραφεν εἰς τὴν γῆν. οἱ δὲ ἀκούσαντες ἐξήρχετο εἷς καθ' εἷς ἀρξάμενοι ἀπὸ τῶν πρεσβυτέρων, καὶ κατελείφθη[23] μόνος, καὶ ἡ γυνὴ ἐν μέσῳ οὖσα. ἀνακύψας[24] δὲ ὁ

---

[1] περιέχω pres act ind 3s, surround, contain

[2] ἀναγκαίως, adv, necessarily

[3] ἐκτίθημι aor pass ptcp m.p.dat., explain, relate, state

[4] ἐπιτηρέω perf mid/pass impv 3s, look out for, consider carefully, take into account

[5] ἔλαιον, ου, τό, olive

[6] ὄρθρος, ου, ὁ, early in the morning, dawn

[7] μοιχεία, ας, ἡ, adultery

[8] καταλαμβάνω perf mid/pass ptcp f.s.acc., attain, seize, catch

[9] καταλαμβάνω perf mid/pass ind 3s, attain, seize, catch

[10] αὐτόφωρος, ον, in the act

[11] μοιχεύω pres mid/pass ptcp f.s.nom., commit adultery

[12] ἐντέλλω aor mid ind 3s, command, order

[13] λιθάζω pres act inf, stone

[14] κατηγορέω pres act inf, accuse

[15] κάτω, adv, down

[16] κύπτω aor act ptcp m.s.nom., bend down

[17] δάκτυλος, ου, ὁ, finger

[18] καταγράφω imp act ind 3s, write, draw

[19] ἐπιμένω imp act ind 3s, remain

[20] ἀνακύπτω aor act ind 3s, stand up

[21] ἀναμάρτητος, ον, without sin

[22] κατακύπτω aor act ptcp m.s.nom., bend down

[23] καταλαμβάνω aor pass ind 3s, catch, seize, to be left (pass)

[24] ἀνακύπτω aor act ptcp m.s.nom., stand up

Ἰησοῦς εἶπεν αὐτῇ Γύναι, ποῦ εἰσίν; οὐδείς σε κατέκρινεν;[1] ἡ δὲ εἶπεν Οὐδείς, κύριε. εἶπεν δὲ ὁ Ἰησοῦς Οὐδὲ ἐγώ σε κατακρίνω·[2] πορεύου, ἀπὸ τοῦ νῦν μηκέτι[3] ἁμάρτανε.

5:1 Παπίας[4] Ἱεραπόλεως[5] ἐπίσκοπος[6] ἀκουστὴς[7] τοῦ θεολόγου[8] Ἰωάννου γενόμενος, Πολυκάρπου[9] δὲ ἑταῖρος,[10] πέντε λόγους κυριακῶν[11] λογίων[12] ἔγραψεν, ἐν οἷς ἀπαρίθμησιν[13] ἀποστόλων ποιούμενος μετὰ Πέτρον καὶ Ἰωάννην, Φίλιππον καὶ Θωμᾶν[14] καὶ Ματθαῖον[15] εἰς μαθητὰς τοῦ Κυρίου ἀνέγραψεν[16] Ἀριστίωνα[17] καὶ Ἰωάννην ἕτερον, ὃν καὶ πρεσβύτερον ἐκάλεσεν. ὥς τινας οἴεσθαι,[18] ὅτι τούτου τοῦ Ἰωάννου εἰσὶν αἱ δύο ἐπιστολαὶ αἱ μικραὶ καὶ καθολικαί,[19] αἱ ἐξ ὀνόματος Ἰωάννου φερόμεναι, διὰ τὸ τοὺς ἀρχαίους[20] τὴν πρώτην μόνην ἐγκρίνειν·[21] τινὲς δὲ καὶ τὴν ἀποκάλυψιν[22] τούτου πλανηθέντες ἐνόμισαν.[23] καὶ Παπίας[24] δὲ περὶ τὴν χιλιονταετηρίδα[25] σφάλλεται,[26] ἐξ οὗ καὶ ὁ Εἰρηναῖος.[27] Παπίας[28] ἐν τῷ δευτέρῳ

---

[1] κατακρίνω imp act ind 3s, condemn

[2] κατακρίνω pres act ind 1s, condemn

[3] μηκέτι, adv, no longer, no more

[4] Παπίας, ου, ὁ, Papias

[5] Ἱεράπολις, εως, ἡ, Hieropolis

[6] ἐπίσκοπος, ου, ὁ, bishop

[7] ἀκουστής, οῦ, ὁ, hearer, disciple

[8] θεολόγος, ου, ὁ, theologian, herald

[9] Πολύκαρπος, ου, ὁ, Polycarp

[10] ἑταῖρος, ου, ὁ, companion

[11] κυριακός, ή, όν, belonging to the Lord

[12] λόγιον, ου, τό, saying

[13] ἀπαρίθμησις, εως, ἡ, counting, list

[14] Θωμᾶς, ᾶ, ὁ, Thomas

[15] Ματθίας, ου, ὁ, Matthias

[16] ἀναγράφω aor act ind 3s, record

[17] Ἀριστίων, ωνος, ὁ, Aristion

[18] οἴομαι pres mid/pass inf, suppose

[19] καθολικός, ή, όν, catholic, general, universal

[20] ἀρχαῖος, αία, αῖον, ancient, old

[21] ἐγκρίνω pres act inf, classify, accept

[22] ἀποκάλυψις, εως, ἡ, revelation, Apocalypse

[23] νομίζω aor act ind 3p, think, suppose

[24] Παπίας, ου, ὁ, Papias

[25] χιλιονταετηρίς, ίδος, ἡ, period of the millennium

[26] σφάλλω pres mid/pass ind 3s, stumble, be in error

[27] Εἰρηναῖος, ου, ὁ, Irenaeus

[28] Παπίας, ου, ὁ, Papias

λόγῳ λέγει ὅτι Ἰωάννης ὁ θεολόγος[1] καὶ Ἰάκωβος ὁ ἀδελφὸς αὐτοῦ ὑπὸ Ἰουδαίων ἀνηρέθησαν.[2] Παπίας[3] ὁ εἰρημένος ἱστόρησεν[4] ὡς παραλαβὼν ἀπὸ τῶν θυγατέρων[5] Φιλίππου, ὅτι Βαρσαβᾶς[6] ὁ καὶ Ἰοῦστος[7] δοκιμαζόμενος[8] ὑπὸ τῶν ἀπίστων[9] ἰὸν[10] ἐχίδνης[11] πιὼν ἐν ὀνόματι τοῦ Χριστοῦ ἀπαθὴς[12] διεφυλάχθη.[13] ἱστορεῖ[14] δὲ καὶ ἄλλα θαύματα[15] καὶ μάλιστα[16] τὸ κατὰ τὴν μητέρα Μαναΐμου[17] τὴν ἐκ νεκρῶν ἀνάστασιν· περὶ τῶν ὑπὸ τοῦ Χριστοῦ ἐκ νεκρῶν ἀναστάντων, ὅτι ἕως Ἀριανοῦ[18] ἔζων.

6:1 Μετὰ δὲ Δομετιανὸν[19] ἐβασίλευσε[20] Νερούας[21] ἔτος ἕν, ὃς ἀνακαλεσάμενος[22] Ἰωάννην ἐκ τῆς νήσου[23] ἀπέλυσεν οἰκεῖν[24] ἐν Ἐφέσῳ.[25] μόνος τότε περιὼν[26] τῷ βίῳ[27] ἐκ τῶν δώδεκα μαθητῶν καὶ συγγραψάμενος[28] τὸ κατ' αὐτὸν εὐαγγέλιον μαρτυρίου[29]

---

[1] θεολόγος, ου, ὁ, theologian, herald
[2] ἀναιρέω aor pass ind 3p, take away, execute
[3] Παπίας, ου, ὁ, Papias
[4] ἱστορέω aor act ind 3s, record
[5] θυγάτηρ, τρός, ἡ, daughter
[6] Βαρσαβᾶς, ᾶ, ὁ, Barsabbas
[7] Ἰοῦστος, ου, ὁ, Justus
[8] δοκιμάζω pres mid/pass ptcp m.s.nom., put to the test
[9] ἄπιστος, ον, unbelieving
[10] ἰός, οῦ, ὁ, poison
[11] ἔχιδνα, ης, ἡ, snake
[12] ἀπαθής, ές, without suffering, unharmed
[13] διαφυλάσσω aor pass ind 3s, protect
[14] ἱστορέω pres act ind 3s, record
[15] θαῦμα, ατος, τό, wonder, amazement

[16] μάλιστα, superl, most of all, especially
[17] Μαναΐμος, ου, Manaimos
[18] Ἀριανός, ου, ὁ, Hadrian
[19] Δομετιανός, ου, ὁ, Domitian
[20] βασιλεύω aor act ind 3s, reign
[21] Νερούας, Nerva
[22] ἀνακαλέω aor mid ptcp m.s.nom., call again, recall
[23] νῆσος, ου, ἡ, island
[24] οἰκέω pres act inf, live
[25] Ἔφεσος, ου, ἡ, Ephesus
[26] περίειμι pres ptcp m.s.nom., be around, survive
[27] βίος, ου, ὁ, life
[28] συγγράφω aor mid ptcp m.s.nom., write
[29] μαρτύριον, ου, τό, testimony, martyrdom

56

κατηξίωται.¹ Παπίας² γὰρ ὁ Ἱεραπόλεως³ ἐπίσκοπος,⁴ αὐτόπτης⁵ τούτου γενόμενος, ἐν τῷ δευτέρῳ λόγῳ τῶν κυριακῶν⁶ λογίων⁷ φάσκει,⁸ ὅτι ὑπὸ Ἰουδαίων ἀνῃρέθη.⁹ πληρώσας δηλαδὴ¹⁰ μετὰ τοῦ ἀδελφοῦ τὴν τοῦ Χριστοῦ περὶ αὐτῶν πρόρρησιν¹¹ καὶ τὴν ἑαυτῶν ὁμολογίαν¹² περὶ τούτου καὶ συγκατάθεσιν·¹³ εἰπὼν γὰρ ὁ Κύριος πρὸς αὐτούς· Δύνασθε πιεῖν τὸ ποτήριον ὃ ἐγὼ πίνω; καὶ κατανευσάντων¹⁴ προθύμως¹⁵ καὶ συνθεμένων·¹⁶ Τὸ ποτήριόν μου, φησίν, πίεσθε καὶ τὸ βάπτισμα¹⁷ ὃ ἐγὼ βαπτίζομαι βαπτισθήσεσθε. καὶ εἰκότως.¹⁸ ἀδύνατον¹⁹ γὰρ Θεὸν ψεύσασθαι.²⁰ **6** οὕτω δὲ καὶ ὁ πολυμαθὴς²¹ Ὠριγένης²² ἐν τῇ κατὰ Ματθαῖον²³ ἑρμηνείᾳ²⁴ διαβεβαιοῦται,²⁵ ὡς ὅτι μεμαρτύρηκεν Ἰωάννης, ἐκ τῶν διαδόχων²⁶ τῶν ἀποστόλων ὑποσημαινάμενος²⁷ τοῦτο μεμαθηκέναι.²⁸ **7** καὶ μὲν δὴ²⁹ καὶ ὁ πολυΐστωρ³⁰ Εὐσέβιος³¹ ἐν τῇ ἐκκλησιαστικῇ³²

¹ καταξιόω perf mid/pass ind 3s, consider worthy, honor
² Παπίας, ου, ὁ, Papias
³ Ἱεράπολις, εως, ἡ, Hierapolis
⁴ ἐπίσκοπος, ου, ὁ, bishop
⁵ αὐτόπτης, ου, ὁ, eyewitness
⁶ κυριακός, ή, όν, belonging to the Lord
⁷ λόγιον, ου, τό, saying
⁸ φάσκω pres act ind 3s, assert
⁹ ἀναιρέω aor pass ind 3s, take away, execute
¹⁰ δηλαδή, adv, plainly
¹¹ πρόρρησις, εως, ἡ, prediction, prophecy
¹² ὁμολογία, ας, ἡ, confession
¹³ συγκατάθεσις, εως, ἡ, agreement
¹⁴ κατανεύω aor act ptcp m.s.nom., signal, nod in agreement, assent
¹⁵ προθύμως, adv, eagerly
¹⁶ συντίθημι aor mid ptcp m.p.gen., place together, agree

¹⁷ βάπτισμα, ατος, τό, baptism
¹⁸ εἰκότως, adv, appropriate, good reason
¹⁹ ἀδύνατος, ον, impossible
²⁰ ψεύδομαι aor pass inf, lie
²¹ πολυμαθής, ές, knowing much, encyclopedic
²² Ὠριγένης, ου, ὁ, Origen
²³ Ματθίας, ου, ὁ, Matthias
²⁴ ἑρμηνεία, ας, ἡ, translation, interpretation
²⁵ διαβεβαιόω pres mid/pass ind 3s, affirm
²⁶ διάδοχος, ου, ὁ, successor
²⁷ ὑποσημαίνω aor mid ind m.s.nom., indicate
²⁸ μανθάνω perf act inf, learn
²⁹ δή, part, then, now, indeed
³⁰ πολυΐστωρ, ορος, ὁ, very learned, well-informed
³¹ Εὐσέβιος, ου, ὁ, Eusebius
³² ἐκκλησιαστικός, ή, όν, church

ἱστορίᾳ[1] φησί· Θωμᾶς[2] μὲν τὴν Παρθίαν[3] εἴληχεν,[4] Ἰωάννης δὲ τὴν Ἀσίαν,[5] πρὸς οὓς καὶ διατρίψας[6] ἐτελεύτησεν[7] ἐν Ἐφέσῳ.[8]

10:1 Περὶ μέντοι[9] τοῦ θεοπνεύστου[10] τῆς βίβλου[11] τῆς ἀποκαλύψεως[12] Ἰωάννου περιττὸν[13] μηκύνειν[14] τὸν λόγον ἡγούμεθα,[15] τῶν μακαρίων Γρηγορίου[16] φημὶ τοῦ θεολόγου[17] καὶ Κυρίλλου,[18] προσέτι[19] δὲ καὶ τῶν ἀρχαιοτέρων[20] Παπίου,[21] Εἰρηναίου,[22] Μεθοδίου[23] καὶ Ἱππολύτου[24] ταύτῃ προσμαρτυρούντων[25] τὸ ἀξιόπιστον.[26]

11:1 Παπίας[27] δὲ οὕτως ἐπὶ λέξεως·[28] Ἐνίοις[29] δὲ αὐτῶν, δηλαδὴ[30] τῶν πάλαι[31] θείων[32] ἀγγέλων, καὶ τῆς περὶ τὴν γῆν διακοσμήσεως[33] ἔδωκεν ἄρχειν καὶ καλῶς ἄρχειν παρηγγύησε.[34]

---

[1] ἱστορία, ας, ἡ, history
[2] Θωμᾶς, ᾶ, ὁ, Thomas
[3] Πάρθος, ου, Parthia
[4] λαγχάνω perf act ind 3s, receive
[5] Ἀσία, ας, ἡ, Asia
[6] διατρίβω aor act ptcp m.s.nom., remain, stay
[7] τελευτάω aor act ind 3s, die
[8] Ἔφεσος, ου, ἡ, Ephesus
[9] μέντοι, conj, though, however
[10] θεόπνευστος, ον, God-breathed, inspired by God
[11] βίβλος, ου, ἡ, book
[12] ἀποκάλυψις, εως, ἡ, revelation, apocalypse
[13] περισσός, ή, όν, extraordinary, superfluous
[14] μηκύνω pres act inf, make long
[15] ἡγέομαι pres mid/pass ind 1p, lead, consider
[16] Γρηγόριος, ου, ὁ, Gregory
[17] θεολόγος, ου, ὁ, theologian, herald

[18] Κύριλλος, ου, ὁ, Cyril
[19] προσέτι, adv, over and above, still more
[20] ἀρχαῖος, αία, αῖον, old, ancient
[21] Παπίας, ου, ὁ, Papias
[22] Εἰρηναῖος, ου, ὁ, Irenaeus
[23] Μεθόδιος, ου, ὁ, Methodius
[24] Ἱππόλυτος, ου, ὁ, Hippolytus
[25] προσμαρτυρέω pres act ptcp m.p.gen., confirm
[26] ἀξιόπιστος, ον, trustworthy, genuine
[27] Παπίας, ου, ὁ, Papias
[28] λέξις, εως, ἡ, speech, expression, word for word
[29] ἔνιοι, αι, α, some
[30] δηλαδή, adv, plainly, clearly
[31] πάλαι, adv, long ago, formerly
[32] θεῖος, θεία, θεῖον, divine, holy
[33] διακόσμησις, εως, ἡ, orderly arrangement
[34] παρεγγυάω aor act ind 3s, command

καὶ ἑξῆς[1] φησίν· Εἰς οὐδὲν δέον[2] συνέβη[3] τελευτῆσαι[4] τὴν τάξιν[5] αὐτῶν. Καὶ ἐβλήθη ὁ δράκων[6] ὁ μέγας, ὁ ὄφις[7] ὁ ἀρχαῖος[8] ὁ καλούμενος διάβολος καὶ ὁ Σατανᾶς, ὁ πλανῶν τὴν οἰκουμένην[9] ὅλην ἐβλήθη εἰς τὴν γῆν, καὶ οἱ ἄγγελοι αὐτοῦ.

12:1 Λαβόντες τὰς ἀφορμὰς[10] ἐκ Παπίου[11] τοῦ πάνυ[12] τοῦ Ἱεραπολίτου,[13] τοῦ ἐν τῷ ἐπιστηθίῳ[14] φοιτήσαντος,[15] καὶ Κλήμεντος,[16] Πανταίνου[17] τῆς Ἀλεξανδρέων[18] ἱερέως καὶ Ἀμμωνίου[19] σοφωτάτου,[20] τῶν ἀρχαίων[21] καὶ πρώτων συνῳδῶν[22] ἐξηγητῶν,[23] εἰς Χριστὸν καὶ τὴν ἐκκλησίαν πᾶσαν τὴν ἑξαήμερον[24] νοησάντων.[25]

13:1 Οἱ μὲν οὖν ἀρχαιότεροι[26] τῶν ἐκκλησιῶν ἐξηγητικῶν,[27] λέγω δὴ[28] Φίλων[29] ὁ φιλόσοφος[30] καὶ τῶν ἀποστόλων ὁμόχρονος[31] καὶ Παπίας[32] ὁ πολὺς ὁ Ἰωάννου τοῦ εὐαγγελιστοῦ[33] φοιτητὴς[34]

---

[1] ἑξῆς, adv, next
[2] δέον, οντος, τό, necessary
[3] συμβαίνω aor act ind 3s, come about
[4] τελευτάω aor act inf, come to an end
[5] τάξις, εως, ἡ, administration
[6] δράκων, οντος, ὁ, dragon
[7] ὄφις, εως, ὁ, serpent
[8] ἀρχαῖος, αία, αῖον, ancient
[9] οἰκουμένη, ης, ἡ, world
[10] ἀφορμή, ῆς, ἡ, starting-point, cue
[11] Παπίας, ου, ὁ, Papias
[12] πάνυ, adv, altogether, very, renowned
[13] Ἱεραπολίτης, ου, ὁ, inhabitant of Hierapolis
[14] ἐπιστήθιος, ου, ὁ, close friend
[15] φοιτάω aor act ptcp m.s.gen., move about, be an intimate of
[16] Κλήμης, εντος, ὁ, Clement
[17] Πανταῖνος, ου, ὁ, Pantaenus
[18] Ἀλεξανδρεύς, έως, ὁ, Alexandrian
[19] Ἀμμώνιος, ου, ὁ, Ammonius
[20] σοφός, ή, όν, superl, wise, learned
[21] ἀρχαῖος, αία, αῖον, ancient
[22] συνῳδός, όν, in agreement
[23] ἐξηγητής, οῦ, ὁ, interpreter
[24] ἑξαήμερος, ον, six days
[25] νοέω aor act ptcp m.p.gen., understand
[26] ἀρχαῖος, αία, αῖον, ancient
[27] ἐξηγητικός, ή, όν, interpretation, interpretor
[28] δή, part, indeed
[29] Φίλων, ωνος, ὁ, Philo
[30] φιλόσοφος, ου, ὁ, philosopher
[31] ὁμόχρονος, ον, contemporaneous
[32] Παπίας, ου, ὁ, Papias
[33] εὐαγγελιστής, οῦ, ὁ, evangelist
[34] φοιτητής, οῦ, ὁ, disciple

ὁ Ἱεραπολίτης,[1] Εἰρηναῖός τε ὁ Λουγδουνεὺς[2] καὶ Ἰουστίνος[3] ὁ μάρτυς καὶ φιλόσοφος,[4] Πανταῖνός[5] τε ὁ Ἀλεξανδρείας[6] καὶ Κλήμης[7] ὁ Στρωματεὺς[8] καὶ οἱ ἀμφ[9] αὐτοὺς πνευματικῶς[10] τὰ περὶ παραδείσου[11] ἐθεώρησαν εἰς τὴν Χριστοῦ ἐκκλησίαν ἀναφερόμενοι.[12]

14:4 Ταῦτα δὲ καὶ Παπίας[13] ὁ Ἰωάννου μὲν ἀκουστής,[14] Πολυκάρπου[15] δὲ ἑταῖρος[16] γεγονώς, ἀρχαῖος[17] ἀνήρ, ἐγγράφως[18] ἐπιμαρτυρεῖ[19] ἐν τῇ τετάρτῃ[20] τῶν ἑαυτοῦ βιβλίων· ἔστι γὰρ αὐτῷ πέντε βιβλία συντεταγμένα.[21]

15:1 Τοὺς κατὰ θεὸν ἀκακίαν[22] ἀσκοῦντας[23] παῖδας[24] ἐκάλουν, ὡς καὶ Παπίας[25] δηλοῖ[26] βιβλίῳ πρώτῳ τῶν κυριακῶν[27] ἐξηγήσεων[28] καὶ Κλήμης[29] ὁ Ἀλεξανδρεὺς[30] ἐν τῷ Παιδαγωγῷ.[31]

---

[1] Ἱεραπολίτης, ου, ὁ, inhabitant of Hierapolis
[2] Λουγδουνεὺς, έως, ὁ, citizen of Lyons
[3] Ἰουστίνος, ου, ὁ, Justin
[4] φιλόσοφος, ου, ὁ, philosopher
[5] Πανταῖνος, ου, ὁ, Pantaenus
[6] Ἀλεξανδρεία, ας, ἡ, Alexandrian
[7] Κλήμης, εντος, ὁ, Clement
[8] Στρωματεύς, έως, ὁ, Stromateus
[9] ἀμφί, prep, on both sides, around
[10] πνευματικῶς, adv, spiritually
[11] παράδεισος, ου, ὁ, paradise
[12] ἀναφέρω pres mid/pass ptcp m.p.nom., lead up, bring up
[13] Παπίας, ου, ὁ, Papias
[14] ἀκουστής, οῦ, ὁ, hearer
[15] Πολύκαρπος, ου, ὁ, Polycarp
[16] ἑταῖρος, ου, ὁ, companion
[17] ἀρχαῖος, αία, αῖον, former times, ancient, early period
[18] ἐγγράφως, adv, in writing
[19] ἐπιμαρτυρέω pres act ind 3s, bear witness
[20] τέταρτος, η, ον, fourth
[21] συντάσσω perf mid/pass ptcp n.p.nom., order, compose
[22] ἀκακία, ας, ἡ, innocence
[23] ἀσκέω pres act ptcp m.p.acc., practice
[24] παῖς, παιδός, ὁ, child
[25] Παπίας, ου, ὁ, Papias
[26] δηλόω pres act ind 3s, make clear, show
[27] κυριακός, ή, όν, belonging to the Lord
[28] ἐξήγησις, εως, ἡ, explanation, exposition
[29] Κλήμης, εντος, ὁ, Clement
[30] Ἀλεξανδρεύς, έως, ὁ, Alexandrian
[31] παιδαγωγός, οῦ, ὁ, guardian, pedagogue

16:1 Ταῦτά φησιν αἰνιττόμενος[1] οἶμαι[2] Παπίαν[3] τὸν Ἱεραπόλεως[4] τῆς κατ᾽ Ἀσίαν[5] τότε γενόμενον ἐπίσκοπον[6] καὶ συνακμάσαντα[7] τῷ θείῳ[8] εὐαγγελιστῇ[9] Ἰωάννῃ. οὗτος γὰρ ὁ Παπίας[10] ἐν τῷ τετάρτῳ[11] αὐτοῦ βιβλίῳ τῶν κυριακῶν[12] ἐξηγήσεων[13] τὰς διὰ βρωμάτων[14] εἶπεν ἐν τῇ ἀναστάσει ἀπολαύσεις·[15] εἰς ὅπερ[16] δόγμα[17] μετὰ ταῦτα ἐπίστευσεν Ἀπολλινάριος,[18] ὃ καλοῦσί τινες χιλιονταετηρίδα[19] καὶ Εἰρηναῖος[20] δὲ ὁ Λουγδούνου[21] ἐν τῷ κατὰ αἱρέσεων[22] πέμπτῳ[23] λόγῳ τὸ αὐτό φησι καὶ παράγει[24] μάρτυρα τῶν ὑπ᾽ αὐτοῦ εἰρημένων τὸν λεχθέντα Παπίαν.[25]

17:1 Οὐ μὴν ἀλλ᾽ οὐδὲ Παπίαν[26] τὸν Ἱεραπόλεως[27] ἐπίσκοπον[28] καὶ μάρτυρα, οὐδὲ Εἰρηναῖον[29] τὸν ὅσιον[30] ἐπίσκοπον[31] Λουγδούνων[32] ἀποδέχεται[33] Στέφανος,[34] ἐν οἷς λέγουσιν

---

[1] αἰνίσσομαι pres mid/pass ptcp m.s.nom., intimate, hint at

[2] οἴομαι pres mid/pass ind 1s, think, suppose

[3] Παπίας, ου, ὁ, Papias

[4] Ἱεράπολις, εως, ἡ, Hierapolis

[5] Ἀσία, ας, ἡ, Asia

[6] ἐπίσκοπος, ου, ὁ, bishop

[7] συνακμάζω aor act ptcp m.s.acc., flourish

[8] θεῖος, θεία, θεῖον, divine, holy

[9] εὐαγγελιστής, οῦ, ὁ, evangelist

[10] Παπίας, ου, ὁ, Papias

[11] τέταρτος, η, ον, fourth

[12] κυριακός, ή, όν, belonging to the Lord

[13] ἐξήγησις, εως, ἡ, explanation, exposition

[14] βρῶμα, ατος, τό, food

[15] ἀπόλαυσις, εως, ἡ, enjoyment

[16] ὅσπερ, ἥπερ, ὅπερ, this very

[17] δόγμα, ατος, τό, ordinance, doctrine

[18] Ἀπολλινάριος, ου, ὁ, Apollinarius

[19] χιλιονταετηρίς, ίδος, ἡ, the millennium

[20] Εἰρηναῖος, ου, ὁ, Irenaeus

[21] Λουγδουνεύς, έως, ὁ, citizen of Lyons

[22] αἵρεσις, έσεως, ἡ, heresy

[23] πέμπτος, η, ον, fifth

[24] παράγω pres act ind 3s, bring in, introduce

[25] Παπίας, ου, ὁ, Papias

[26] Παπίας, ου, ὁ, Papias

[27] Ἱεράπολις, εως, ἡ, Hierapolis

[28] ἐπίσκοπος, ου, ὁ, bishop

[29] Εἰρηναῖος, ου, ὁ, Irenaeus

[30] ὅσιος, ία, ον, devout, holy

[31] ἐπίσκοπος, ου, ὁ, bishop

[32] Λουγδουνεύς, έως, ὁ, citizen of Lyons

[33] ἀποδέχομαι pres mid/pass ind 3s, welcome, accept, follow

[34] Στέφανος, ου, ὁ, Stephen

αἰσθητῶν[1] τινῶν βρωμάτων[2] ἀπόλαυσιν[3] εἶναι τὴν τῶν οὐρανῶν βασιλείαν.

18:1 Ἀπολιναρίου.[4] Οὐκ ἀπέθανε[5] τῇ ἀγχόνῃ[6] Ἰούδας, ἀλλ' ἐπεβίω[7] καθαιρεθεὶς[8] πρὸ τοῦ ἀποπνιγῆναι.[9] καὶ τοῦτο δηλοῦσιν[10] αἱ τῶν ἀποστόλων πράξεις,[11] ὅτι πρηνὴς[12] γενόμενος ἐλάκησε[13] μέσος, καὶ ἐξεχύθη[14] τὰ σπλάγχνα[15] αὐτοῦ. τοῦτο δὲ σαφέστερον[16] ἱστορεῖ[17] Παπίας[18] ὁ Ἰωάννου μαθητὴς λέγων οὕτως ἐν τῷ τετάρτῳ[19] τῆς ἐξηγήσεως[20] τῶν κυριακῶν[21] λόγων·

Μέγα δὲ ἀσεβείας[22] ὑπόδειγμα[23] ἐν τούτῳ τῷ κόσμῳ περιεπάτησεν ὁ Ἰούδας πρησθεὶς[24] ἐπὶ τοσοῦτον[25] τὴν σάρκα, ὥστε μηδὲ ὁπόθεν[26] ἅμαξα[27] ῥᾳδίως[28] διέρχεται ἐκεῖνον δύνασθαι διελθεῖν, ἀλλὰ μηδὲ αὐτὸν μόνον τὸν τῆς κεφαλῆς ὄγκον[29] αὐτοῦ. τὰ μὲν γὰρ βλέφαρα[30] τῶν ὀφθαλμῶν αὐτοῦ φασὶ

---

[1] αἰσθητός, ή, όν, sensible, perceptible
[2] βρῶμα, ατος, τό, food
[3] ἀπόλαυσις, εως, ἡ, enjoyment
[4] Ἀπολιναρίου, ου, ὁ, Apollinarius
[5] ἀποθνήσκω aor act ind 3s, die
[6] ἀγχόνη, ἡ, hanging
[7] ἐπιβιόω aor act ind 1s, live after, survive
[8] καθαιρέω aor pass ptcp m.s.nom., take down
[9] ἀποπνίγω aor pass inf, choke to death
[10] δηλόω pres act ind 3p, make clear
[11] πρᾶξις, εως, ἡ, act
[12] πρηνής, ές, head first
[13] λακάω aor act ind 3s, burst open
[14] ἐκχύνω aor pass ind 3s, pour out
[15] σπλάγχνον, ου, τό, inward parts, entrails

[16] σαφής, comp, clearly
[17] ἱστορέω pres act ind 3s, recount
[18] Παπίας, ου, ὁ, Papias
[19] τέταρτος, η, ον, fourth
[20] ἐξήγησις, εως, ἡ, explanation, exposition
[21] κυριακός, ή, όν, belonging to the Lord
[22] ἀσέβεια, ας, ἡ, ungodliness
[23] ὑπόδειγμα, ατος, τό, example
[24] πρήθω aor pass ptcp m.s.nom., swell up
[25] τοσοῦτος, αύτη, οῦτον, so much, so great
[26] ὁπόθεν, adv, where
[27] ἅμαξα, ης, ἡ, wagon
[28] ῥᾳδίως, adv, readily, easily
[29] ὄγκος, ου, ὁ, bulk
[30] βλέφαρον, ου, τό, eyelid

τοσοῦτον[1] ἐξοιδῆσαι,[2] ὡς αὐτὸν μὲν καθόλου[3] τὸ φῶς μὴ βλέπειν, τοὺς ὀφθαλμοὺς δὲ αὐτοῦ μηδὲ ὑπὸ ἰατροῦ[4] διὰ διόπτρας[5] ὀφθῆναι δύνασθαι· τοσοῦτον[6] βάθος[7] εἶχον ἀπὸ τῆς ἔξωθεν[8] ἐπιφανείας.[9] τὸ δὲ αἰδοῖον[10] αὐτοῦ πάσης μὲν ἀσχημοσύνης[11] ἀηδέστερον[12] καὶ μεῖζον φαίνεσθαι, φέρεσθαι δὲ δι' αὐτοῦ ἐκ παντὸς τοῦ σώματος συρρέοντας[13] ἰχῶράς[14] τε καὶ σκώληκας[15] εἰς ὕβριν[16] δ' αὐτῶν μόνων τῶν ἀναγκαίων.[17] μετὰ πολλὰς δὲ βασάνους[18] καὶ τιμωρίας[19] ἐν ἰδίῳ, φασί, χωρίῳ[20] τελευτήσαντος,[21] ἀπὸ τῆς ὀδμῆς[22] ἔρημον καὶ ἀοίκητον[23] τὸ χωρίον[24] μέχρι[25] τῆς νῦν γενέσθαι, ἀλλ' οὐδὲ μέχρι[26] τῆς σήμερον δύνασθαί τινα ἐκεῖνον τὸν τόπον παρελθεῖν,[27] ἐὰν μὴ τὰς ῥῖνας[28] ταῖς χερσὶν ἐπιφράξῃ.[29] τοσαύτη[30] διὰ τῆς σαρκὸς αὐτοῦ καὶ ἐπὶ τῆς γῆς ἔκρυσις[31] ἐχώρησεν.[32]

---

[1] τοσοῦτος, αύτη, οῦτον, so much, so great
[2] ἐξοιδέω aor act inf, swell up
[3] καθόλου, adv, entirely
[4] ἰατρός, οῦ, ὁ, physician
[5] διόπτρα, ας, ἡ, optical instrument
[6] τοσοῦτος, αύτη, οῦτον, so much, so great
[7] βάθος, ους, τό, depth, below the surface
[8] ἔξωθεν, adv, outside, outer
[9] ἐπιφάνεια, ας, ἡ, appearance, surface
[10] αἰδοῖον, ου, τό, private parts, genitals
[11] ἀσχημοσύνη, ης, ἡ, shameless, unbecoming
[12] ἀηδής, ές, unpleasant
[13] συρρέω pres act ptcp m.s.acc., flow together
[14] ἰχώρ, ῶρος, ὁ, discharge, push
[15] σκώληξ, ηκος, ὁ, worm

[16] ὕβρις, εως, ἡ, insolence, shame
[17] ἀναγκαῖος, α, ον, applying force
[18] βάσανος, ου, ἡ, torment, agony
[19] τιμωρία, ας, ἡ, punishment
[20] χωρίον, ου, τό, place
[21] τελευτάω aor act ptcp m.s.gen., die
[22] ὀσμή, ῆς, ἡ, odor, stench
[23] ἀοίκητος, ον, uninhabited
[24] χωρίον, ου, τό, place
[25] μέχρι, prep, until
[26] μέχρι, prep, until
[27] παρέρχομαι aor act inf, pass by
[28] ῥίς, ῥινός, ἡ, nose
[29] ἐπιφράσσω aor act sub 3s, close
[30] τοσοῦτος, αύτη, οῦτον, so much, so great
[31] ἔκρυσις, εως, ἡ, outflow, discharge
[32] χωρέω aor act ind 3s, reach, spread

20:1 Ὕστατος[1] γὰρ τούτων Ἰωάννης ὁ τῆς βροντῆς[2] υἱὸς μετακληθείς,[3] πάνυ[4] γηραλέου[5] αὐτοῦ γενομένου, ὡς παρέδοσαν ἡμῖν ὅ τε Εἰρηναῖος[6] καὶ Εὐσέβιος[7] καὶ ἄλλοι πιστοὶ κατὰ διαδοχὴν[8] γεγονότες ἱστορικοί,[9] κατ᾽ ἐκεῖνο καιροῦ αἱρέσεων[10] ἀναφυεισῶν[11] δεινῶν[12] ὑπηγόρευσε[13] τὸ εὐαγγέλιον τῷ ἑαυτοῦ μαθητῇ Παπίᾳ[14] εὐβιώτῳ[15] τῷ Ἱεραπολίτῃ,[16] πρὸς ἀναπλήρωσιν[17] τῶν πρὸ αὐτοῦ κηρυξάντων τὸν λόγον τοῖς ἀνὰ[18] πᾶσαν τὴν οἰκουμένην[19] ἔθνεσιν.

---

[1] ὕστερος, α, ον, superl, later, last
[2] βροντή, ῆς, ἡ, thunder
[3] μετακαλέω aor pass ptcp m.s.nom., call
[4] πάνυ, adv, very
[5] γηραλέος, α, ον, aged
[6] Εἰρηναῖος, ου, ὁ, Irenaeus
[7] Εὐσέβιος, ου, ὁ, Eusebius
[8] διαδοχή, ῆς, ἡ, succession
[9] ἱστορικός, ή, όν, historian
[10] αἵρεσις, έσεως, ἡ, heresy

[11] ἀναφύω aor pass ptcp f.p.gen., spring up
[12] δεινός, ή, όν, terrible
[13] ὑπαγορεύω aor act ind 3s, dictate
[14] Παπίας, ου, ὁ, Papias
[15] εὐβίωτος, ου, ὁ, virtuous
[16] Ἱεραπολίτης, ου, ὁ, inhabitant of Hieropolis
[17] ἀναπλήρωσις, εως, ἡ, filling up
[18] ἀνά, adv, each
[19] οἰκουμένη, ῆς, ἡ, world

Diognetus
APOSTOLIC FATHERS GREEK READER

DIOGNETUS

AN INTRODUCTION

By and large, the writings of the New Testament era as well as those from the period immediately following (i.e., the works of the so-called Apostolic Fathers[1]) are concerned with establishing the faith and discipline of Christian communities. They are works that generally address those within the fold of Christianity. After AD 150, there is a noticeable shift in the orientation of Christian literature. There is now a significant stress on apologetics; that is, a genre of literature that presents reasons for holding to the Christian faith, attempts to answer the ridicule and objections of unbelievers, and attacks on alternative world-views in the Græco-Roman world. Although *The Letter to Diognetus* is classified among the Apostolic Fathers, by genre it is actually part of apologetic literature. This class of writings is thus probably to be dated to the latter half of the second century.[2] Avery Dulles has rightly described this letter as "the pearl of early Christian apologetics."[3] *In nuce*, this anonymous work is the joyous expression in Pauline terms of a man who stands utterly amazed at the gracious revelation of God's love in the death of his Son for sinners.

The original authorship of the letter is now lost to us. From the elegant Greek of the treatise, it is probably correct to observe that the

---

[1] See Clare K. Rothschild, "On the Invention of *Patres Apostolici*," in *New Essays on the Apostolic Fathers*, WUNT 375 (Tübingen: Mohr Siebeck, 2007), 7–34; David Lincicum, "Paratextual Invention of the Term 'Apostolic Fathers,'" *JTS* 66 (2015): 139–48.

[2] For this dating, see Robert M. Grant, *Greek Apologists of the Second Century* (Philadelphia: Westminster Press, 1988), 178–79; Theofried Baumeister, "Zur Datierung der Schrift an Diognet," *Vigiliae Christianae* 42 (1988): 105–11; W. S. Walford, *Epistle to Diognetus* (London: James Nisbet & Co., 1908), 7–9; and L. W. Barnard, "The Enigma of the Epistle to Diognetus," in *Studies in the Apostolic Fathers and Their Background* (New York: Shocken Books, 1966), 172–73, would date it no later than 140.

[3] *A History of Apologetics* (Philadelphia: Westminster Press, 1971), 28.

author experienced a classical education and "possessed considerable literary skill and style." Equally lost is the historical and geographical context of the work and audience.[1] Also noteworthy are three major gaps in the text, at 7.7; 10.1; and 10.8. The last of these lacunae is the most serious for it comes right at the conclusion of the treatise, and so how the text actually ends is not known. This accords with the opinion of most scholars that Diogn. 11 and 12 are a separate work by a different author.

In the first chapter of the treatise, the author notes that Diognetus is interested in learning about the Christian faith. In fact, he has three specific questions that he wants answered. The first question is multifaceted: Who is the God that is worshipped by the Christians, such that they reject the reverence paid to the Græco-Roman deities, does no one practice the distinctive features of Judaism, and in sum, are none afraid to be viewed as nonconformists? Second, why do Christians love each other the way they do? And finally, why has Christianity only recently appeared on the scene of history?

The first question is rooted in the frequent accusation made against the early Christians that they were "atheists," since they refused to worship the Greek and Roman gods. However, the question also seeks to understand the differentiation of Christianity from Judaism—an indication that the difference between church and synagogue was readily apparent to outsiders[2]—and how the worship of the Christian God could have such remarkable fruit: a determination to live above the fashion of the world and a refusal to fear death. The latter is probably a response to having seen or heard of Christians who had died as

---

[1] For some speculation as to the identity of Diognetus, see the discussion of Dulles, *History of Apologetics*, 28–9. Charles E. Hill, *From the Lost Teaching of Polycarp: Identifying Irenaeus' Apostolic Presbyter and the Author of* Ad Diognetum, WUNT 186 (Tübingen: Mohr Siebeck, 2006), has argued for Polycarp as the author. As proof of his thesis that Polycarp is the author of Diogn., Hill points to the way that the author describes himself in Diogn. 11–12, which dovetails with the description of Polycarp elsewhere. Hill finds further evidence in the similarity of themes between Pol. *Phil.* and Mart. Pol., on the one hand, and Diogn., on the other.

[2] This was not the case in the era of the New Testament. See, for instance, Acts 18:12–16.

martyrs. The author's answer to this question and its sub-points occupies him in Diogn. 2–8.

The second question—asking about the source of the love Christians had for one another—reflects an observation not infrequently made by those outside of Christian communities yet familiar to some degree with them. These pagans were struck by the way that these early Christian communities were communities of love, something quite different from their own experience of social relationships. Diognetus 10 seeks to answer this query.

The third question has its basis in Græco-Roman reverence for antiquity. What was true had to be ancient. If it was recent, it was suspect.[1] Thus, if Christianity was true, why had the ancients of the Græco-Roman world not known of it? The recent origin of Christianity thus posed a significant stumbling-block for acceptance of its truth claims. Theophilus of Antioch, in his apologetic work *To Autolycus* also mentions this charge being hurled against the Christian faith.[2] The author devotes some of Chapter 8 and then Chapter 9 to answering this question.

As Markus Bockmuehl has noted, the theological center of the Letter to Diognetus is found in chapters 7–9.[3] Having developed a high Christology in Diogn. 7 in his delineation of the nature of the Christian God, the author now explains the recent appearance of Christianity in terms of a soteriological affirmation that is deeply indebted to Pauline and Petrine categories of thought about the cross as a place of substitution, justification, and imputation. And in these

---

[1] Stephen Benko, *Pagan Rome and the Early Christians* (Bloomington: Indiana University Press, 1984), 21–22; Wolfram Kinzig, "The Idea of Progress in the Early Church until the Age of Constantine," *Studia Patristica* 24 (1993): 123–25.

[2] *To Autolycus* 3.4. After mentioning such charges against Christianity as incest and cannibalism, Theophlius notes a third charge, that of Christianity being novel: "They also say that our message has been made public only recently, and that we have nothing to say in proof of our truth and our teaching; they call our message foolishness" (trans. Robert M. Grant in his ed., *Theophilus of Antioch: Ad Autolycum* [Oxford: Clarendon, 1970], 105).

[3] Markus Bockmuehl, *Revelation and Mystery in Ancient Judaism and Pauline Christianity* (Grand Rapids: Eerdmans, 1997), 219.

chapters the author's deep sense of joy for what God has done for humanity in Christ especially comes to the fore. His Pauline crucicentrism is thus interwoven with praise and doxology as he thinks about the cross: "O the sweet exchange! O the inscrutable work of God! O blessings beyond all expectation!"[1]

Diognetus 11–12 are probably best seen as a separate text: they are a homiletical reflection on the Christ as the Word and the tree of knowledge in the Garden of Eden.

Michael A. G. Haykin

---

[1] Diogn. 9.5.

ΕΠΙΣΤΟΛΗ
ΠΡΟΣ ΔΙΟΓΝΗΤΟΝ

NOTES BY MATTHEW ALBANESE

Ἡ ἐκκλησία τοῦ θεοῦ ἡ παροικοῦσα[1] Σμύρναν

1:1 ᾽ΕΠΕΙΔΗ[2] ὁρῶ, κράτιστε[3] Διόγνητε,[4] ὑπερεσπουδακότα[5] σε τὴν θεοσέβειαν[6] τῶν Χριστιανῶν μαθεῖν[7] καὶ πάνυ[8] σαφῶς[9] καὶ ἐπιμελῶς[10] πυνθανόμενον[11] περὶ αὐτῶν, τίνι τε Θεῷ πεποιθότες καὶ πῶς θρησκεύοντες[12] αὐτὸν τόν τε κόσμον ὑπερορῶσι[13] πάντες καὶ θανάτου καταφρονοῦσι,[14] καὶ οὔτε τοὺς νομιζομένους[15] ὑπὸ τῶν Ἑλλήνων[16] θεοὺς λογίζονται οὔτε τὴν ᾽Ιουδαίων δεισιδαιμονίαν[17] φυλάσσουσι, καὶ τίνα τὴν φιλοστοργίαν[18] ἔχουσι πρὸς ἀλλήλους, καὶ τί δήποτε[19] καινὸν τοῦτο γένος[20] ἢ ἐπιτήδευμα[21] εἰσῆλθεν εἰς τὸν βίον[22] νῦν καὶ οὐ

---

[1] παροικέω pres act ptcp f.s.nom., inhabit a place as a foreigner, be a stranger

[2] ἐπειδή, conj, when, after

[3] κράτιστος, η, ον, superl, most noble, most excellent

[4] Διόγνητος, ου, ὁ, Diognetus

[5] ὑπερσπουδάζω perf act ptcp m.s.acc., take great pains, be very eager

[6] θεοσέβεια, ας, ἡ, piety, godliness

[7] μανθάνω aor act inf, learn

[8] πάνυ, adv, altogether, very

[9] σαφῶς, adv, clearly, exactly, very well

[10] ἐπιμελῶς, adv, carefully, diligently

[11] πυνθάνομαι pres mid/pass part m.s.acc., inquire, ask, learn

[12] θρησκεύω pres act ptcp m.p.nom., worship

[13] ὑπεροράω pres act ind 3p, disdain, despise, disregard

[14] καταφρονέω pres act ind 3p, look down on

[15] νομίζω pres mid/pass ptcp m.p.acc., think, believe, consider

[16] Ἕλλην, ηνος, ὁ, Greek

[17] δεισιδαιμονία, ας, ἡ, religious, religion

[18] φιλοστοργία, ας, ἡ, heartfelt love, strong affection

[19] δήποτε, adv, at any time

[20] γένος, ους, τό, descendant, people, class

[21] ἐπιτήδευμα, ατος, τό, pursuit, way of living

[22] βίος, ου, ὁ, life

πρότερον;¹ **2** ἀποδέχομαί² γε³ τῆς προθυμίας⁴ σε ταύτης καὶ παρὰ τοῦ Θεοῦ, τοῦ καὶ τὸ λέγειν καὶ τὸ ἀκούειν ἡμῖν χορηγοῦντος,⁵ αἰτοῦμαι δοθῆναι ἐμοὶ μὲν εἰπεῖν οὕτως ὡς μάλιστα⁶ ἂν ἀκούσαντά σε βελτίω⁷ γενέσθαι, σοί τε οὕτως ἀκοῦσαι ὡς μὴ λυπηθῆναι⁸ τὸν εἰπόντα.

2:1 Ἄγε δή,⁹ καθάρας¹⁰ σεαυτὸν ἀπὸ πάντων τῶν προκατεχόντων¹¹ σου τὴν διάνοιαν¹² λογισμῶν,¹³ καὶ τὴν ἀπατῶσάν¹⁴ σε συνήθειαν¹⁵ ἀποσκευασάμενος,¹⁶ καὶ γενόμενος ὥσπερ ἐξ ἀρχῆς καινὸς ἄνθρωπος, ὡς ἂν καὶ λόγου καινοῦ, καθάπερ¹⁷ καὶ αὐτὸς ὡμολόγησας,¹⁸ ἀκροατὴς¹⁹ ἐσόμενος· ἴδε²⁰ μὴ μόνον τοῖς ὀφθαλμοῖς ἀλλὰ καὶ τῇ φρονήσει²¹ τίνος ὑποστάσεως²² ἢ τίνος εἴδους²³ τυγχάνουσιν²⁴ οὓς ἐρεῖτε καὶ νομίζετε²⁵ Θεούς. **2** οὐχ ὁ μέν τις λίθος ἐστὶν ὅμοιος τῷ

---

¹ πρότερος, α, ον, former, earlier
² ἀποδέχομαι pres mid/pass ind 1s, welcome, accept
³ γέ, part, at least, even, indeed
⁴ προθυμία, ας, ἡ, willingness, readiness, goodwill
⁵ χορηγέω pres act ptcp m.s.gen., provide, supply
⁶ μάλιστα, superl, most of all, above all
⁷ βελτίων, ον, superl, better
⁸ λυπέω aor pass inf, vex, irritate, offend, insult
⁹ δή, part, indeed, now
¹⁰ καθαίρω aor act ptcp m.s.nom., make clean
¹¹ προκατέχω pres act ptcp m.p.gen., gain possession of previously, occupy previously
¹² διάνοια, ας, ἡ, understanding, mind, thought
¹³ λογισμός, οῦ, ὁ, reasoning, reasoning power, wisdom

¹⁴ ἀπατάω pres act ptcp f.s.acc., deceive, mislead
¹⁵ συνήθεια, ας, ἡ, friendship, fellowship, intimacy,
¹⁶ ἀποσκευάζω aor mid ptcp m.s.nom., lay aside, get rid of
¹⁷ καθάπερ, conj, just as
¹⁸ ὁμολογέω aor act ind 2s, promise, confess
¹⁹ ἀκροατής, οῦ, ὁ, a hearer
²⁰ ἴδε, interj, look!, see!
²¹ φρόνησις, εως, ἡ, way of thinking, (frame of) mind
²² ὑπόστασις, εως, ἡ, substantial nature, essence
²³ εἶδος, ους, τό, form, outward appearance
²⁴ τυγχάνω pres act ind 3p, meet, find
²⁵ νομίζω pres act ind 2p, have in common use, think

πατουμένῳ,[1] ὁ δ' ἐστὶ χαλκὸς[2] οὐ κρείσσων[3] τῶν εἰς τὴν χρῆσιν[4] ἡμῖν κεχαλκευμένων[5] σκευῶν,[6] ὁ δὲ ξύλον[7] ἤδη καὶ σεσηπός,[8] ὁ δὲ ἄργυρος[9] χρήζων[10] ἀνθρώπου τοῦ φυλάξαντος ἵνα μὴ κλαπῇ,[11] ὁ δὲ σίδηρος[12] ὑπὸ ἰοῦ[13] διεφθαρμένος,[14] ὁ δὲ ὄστρακον,[15] οὐδὲν τοῦ κατεσκευασμένου[16] πρὸς τὴν ἀτιμοτάτην[17] ὑπηρεσίαν εὐπρεπέστερον;[18] **3** οὐ φθαρτῆς[19] ὕλης[20] ταῦτα πάντα; οὐχ ὑπὸ σιδήρου[21] καὶ πυρὸς κεχαλκευμένα;[22] οὐχ ὁ μὲν αὐτῶν λιθοξόος[23] ὁ δὲ χαλκεὺς[24] ὁ δὲ ἀργυροκόπος[25] ὁ δὲ κεραμεὺς[26] ἔπλασεν;[27] οὐ πρὶν[28] ἢ ταῖς τέχναις[29] τούτων εἰς τὴν μορφὴν[30] ταύτην ἐκτυπωθῆναι[31] ἣν ἕκαστον αὐτῶν ἑκάστῳ εἰκάζειν[32] μεταμεμορ-

---

[1] πατέω pres mid/pass ptcp m.s.dat., tread, walk, trample

[2] χαλκός, οῦ, ὁ, brass, bronze

[3] κρείττων, ον, more prominent, higher in rank

[4] χρῆσις, εως, ἡ, use, usage, usefulness

[5] χαλκεύω perf mid/pass ptcp n.p.gen., forge

[6] σκεῦος, ους, τό, thing, object, vessel

[7] ξύλον, ου, τό, wood, tree

[8] σήπω perf act ptcp n.s.nom., decay, rot

[9] ἄργυρος, ου, ὁ, silver, money

[10] χρήζω pres act ptcp m.s.nom., need, (have) need (of)

[11] κλέπτω aor pass sub 3s, steal

[12] σίδηρος, ου, ὁ, iron

[13] ἰός, οῦ, ὁ, poison, venom, corrosion, rust

[14] διαφθείρω perf mid/pass ptcp m.s.nom., spoil, destroy, deprave, ruin

[15] ὄστρακον, ου, τό, baked clay, pottery

[16] κατασκευάζω perf mid/pass ptcp m.s.gen., make ready

[17] ἄτιμος, ον, superl, dishonored, despised, insignificant

[18] εὐπρεπής, ές, looking well, suited

[19] φθαρτός, ή, όν, perishable

[20] ὕλη, ης, ἡ, forest, wood, material

[21] σίδηρος, ου, ὁ, iron

[22] χαλκεύω perf mid/pass ptcp n.p.nom., forge

[23] λιθοξόος, ου, ὁ, sculptor

[24] χαλκεύς, έως, ὁ, (black)smith, metalworker

[25] ἀργυροκόπος, ου, ὁ, silversmith

[26] κεραμεύς, έως, ὁ, potter

[27] πλάσσω aor act ind 3s, form, mold, shape

[28] πρίν, conj/adv, before

[29] τέχνη, ης, ἡ, skill, trade

[30] μορφή, ῆς, ἡ, form, outward appearance, shape

[31] ἐκτυπόω aor pass inf, shape

[32] εἰκάζω pres act inf, suppose, imagine

φωμένον;[1] οὐ τὰ νῦν ἐκ τῆς αὐτῆς ὕλης[2] ὄντα σκεύη[3] γένοιτ' ἄν, εἰ τύχοι[4] τῶν αὐτῶν τεχνιτῶν,[5] ὅμοια τοιούτοις; **4** οὐ ταῦτα πάλιν τὰ νῦν ὑφ' ὑμῶν προσκυνούμενα δύναιτ' ἂν ὑπὸ ἀνθρώπων σκεύη[6] ὅμοια γενέσθαι τοῖς λοιποῖς; οὐ κωφὰ[7] πάντα, οὐ τυφλά, οὐκ ἄψυχα,[8] οὐκ ἀναίσθητα,[9] οὐκ ἀκίνητα;[10] οὐ πάντα σηπόμενα,[11] οὐ πάντα φθειρόμενα.[12] **5** ταῦτα Θεοὺς καλεῖτε, τούτοις δουλεύετε,[13] τούτοις προσκυνεῖτε· τέλεον[14] δ' αὐτοῖς ἐξομοιοῦσθε. [15] **6** διὰ τοῦτο μισεῖτε Χριστιανούς,[16] ὅτι τούτους οὐχ ἡγοῦνται[17] θεούς. **7** ὑμεῖς γὰρ οἱ νῦν νομίζοντες[18] καὶ σεβόμενοι,[19] οὐ πολὺ πλέον αὐτῶν καταφρονεῖτε;[20] οὐ πολὺ μᾶλλον αὐτοὺςχλευάζετε[21] καὶ ὑβρίζετε,[22] τοὺς μὲν λιθίνους[23] καὶ ὀστρακίνους[24] σέβοντες[25] ἀφυλάκτως,[26] τοὺς δὲ ἀργυρέους[27] καὶ

---

[1] μεταμορφόω perf mid/pass ptcp n.s.acc., be transfigured, be changed, be transformed
[2] ὕλη, ης, ἡ, forest, wood, material
[3] σκεῦος, ους, τό, thing, object, vessel
[4] τυγχάνω aor act opt 3s, meet, find
[5] τεχνίτης, ου, ὁ, craftsperson, artisan, designer
[6] σκεῦος, ους, τό, thing, object, vessel
[7] κωφός, ή, όν, mute, deaf
[8] ἄψυχος, ον, inanimate, lifeless
[9] ἀναίσθητος, ον, without feeling/perception
[10] ἀκίνητος, ον, immovable, unable to move
[11] σήπω pres mid/pass ptcp n.p.nom., decay, rot
[12] φθείρω pres mid/pass ptcp n.p.nom., destroy, ruin, corrupt
[13] δουλεύω pres act ind 2p, be a slave, be subjected
[14] τέλειος, α, ον, perfect, complete, mature

[15] ἐξομοιόω pres mid/pass ind 3p, become just like/similar
[16] Χριστιανός, οῦ, ὁ, Christ-partisan, Christian
[17] ἡγέομαι pres mid/pass ind 3p, lead, guide, think
[18] νομίζω pres act ptcp m.p.nom., have in common use, think
[19] σέβω pres mid/pass ptcp m.p.nom., worship, show reverence/respect for
[20] καταφρονέω pres act impv 2p, look down on, despise
[21] χλευάζω pres act ind 2p, mock, sneer, scoff
[22] ὑβρίζω pres act ind 2p, mistreat, insult
[23] λίθινος, ίνη, ον, (made of) stone
[24] ὀστράκινος, η, ον, made of earth/clay
[25] σέβω pres act ptcp m.p.nom., worship, show reverence/respect for
[26] ἀφυλάκτως, adv, without guarding
[27] ἀργυροῦς, ᾶ, οῦν, silver

χρυσοῦς[1] ἐγκλείοντες[2] ταῖς νυξί, καὶ ταῖς ἡμέραις φύλακας[3] παρακαθιστάντες,[4] ἵνα μὴ κλαπῶσιν;[5] **8** αἷς δὲ δοκεῖτε τιμαῖς προσφέρειν, εἰ μὲν αἰσθάνονται,[6] κολάζετε[7] μᾶλλον αὐτούς· εἰ δὲ ἀναισθητοῦσιν,[8] ἐλέγχοντες[9] αἵματι καὶ κνίσαις[10] αὐτοὺς θρησκεύετε.[11] **9** ταῦθ᾽ ὑμῶν τις ὑπομεινάτω,[12] ταῦτα ἀνασχέσθω[13] τις ἑαυτῷ γενέσθαι. ἀλλὰ ἄνθρωπος μὲν οὐδὲ εἷς ταύτης τῆς κολάσεως[14] ἑκὼν[15] ἀνέξεται,[16] αἴσθησιν[17] γὰρ ἔχει καὶ λογισμόν.[18] ὁ δὲ λίθος ἀνέχεται,[19] ἀναισθητεῖ[20] γάρ· οὐκοῦν[21] τὴν αἴσθησιν[22] αὐτοῦ ἐλέγχετε.[23] **10** περὶ μὲν οὖν τοῦ μὴ δεδουλῶσθαι[24] Χριστιανοὺς[25] τοιούτοις θεοῖς πολλὰ μὲν ἂν καὶ ἄλλα εἰπεῖν ἔχοιμι· εἰ δέ τινι μὴ δοκοίη κἂν ταῦτα ἱκανά, περισσὸν[26] ἡγοῦμαι[27] καὶ τὸ πλείω λέγειν.

---

[1] χρυσός, οῦ, ὁ, gold, coined gold, money

[2] ἐγκλείω pres act ptcp m.p.nom., lock up, shut up, enclose

[3] φύλαξ, ακος, ὁ, guard, sentinel

[4] παρακαθίστημι pres act ptcp m.p.nom., post

[5] κλέπτω aor pass sub 3p, steal

[6] αἰσθάνομαι pres mid/pass ind 3p, notice, understand

[7] κολάζω pres act ind 2p, penalize, punish

[8] ἀναισθητέω pres act ind 3p, be unfeeling, insensible

[9] ἐλέγχω pres act ptcp m.p.nom., bring to light

[10] κνῖσα, ης, ἡ, the odor of burning fat

[11] θρησκεύω pres act ind 2p, worship

[12] ὑπομένω aor act impv 3s, endure

[13] ἀνέχω aor mid impv 3s, endure, bear with

[14] κόλασις, εως, ἡ, punishment

[15] ἑκών, οῦσα, όν, willing(ly), glad(ly)

[16] ἀνέχω fut mid ind 3s, endure, bear with

[17] αἴσθησις, εως, ἡ, perception, sensation, discernment

[18] λογισμός, οῦ, ὁ, reasoning, wisdom

[19] ἀνέχω pres mid/pass ind 3s, endure, bear with

[20] ἀναισθητέω pres act ind 3s be unfeeling, insensible

[21] οὐκοῦν, conj, therefore, so

[22] αἴσθησις, εως, ἡ, perception, discernment

[23] ἐλέγχω pres act ind 2p, expose

[24] δουλόω perf mid/pass inf, enslave, cause to be like a slave

[25] Χριστιανός, οῦ, ὁ Christ-partisan, Christian

[26] περισσός, ή, όν, extraordinary, remarkable

[27] ἡγέομαι pres mid/pass ind 1s, lead, guide

3:1 Ἑξῆς¹ δὲ περὶ τοῦ μὴ κατὰ τὰ αὐτὰ Ἰουδαίοις θεοσεβεῖν² αὐτοὺς οἶμαί³ σε μάλιστα⁴ ποθεῖν⁵ ἀκοῦσαι. **2** Ἰουδαῖοι τοίνυν,⁶ εἰ μὲν ἀπέχονται⁷ ταύτης τῆς προειρημένης⁸ λατρείας,⁹ καλῶς Θεὸν ἕνα τῶν πάντων σέβειν¹⁰ καὶ δεσπότην¹¹ ἀξιοῦσι¹² φρονεῖν·¹³ εἰ δὲ τοῖς προειρημένοις¹⁴ ὁμοιοτρόπως¹⁵ τὴν θρησκείαν¹⁶ προσάγουσιν¹⁷ αὐτῷ ταύτην, διαμαρτάνουσιν.¹⁸ **3** ἃ γὰρ τοῖς ἀναισθήτοις¹⁹ καὶ κωφοῖς²⁰ προσφέροντες οἱ Ἕλληνες²¹ ἀφροσύνης²² δεῖγμα²³ παρέχουσι,²⁴ ταῦθ' οὗτοι, καθάπερ²⁵ προσδεομένῳ²⁶ τῷ Θεῷ λογιζόμενοι παρέχειν,²⁷ μωρίαν²⁸ εἰκός²⁹ μᾶλλον ἡγοῖντ'³⁰ ἄν, οὐ θεοσέβειαν.³¹ **4** ὁ γὰρ ποιήσας τὸν οὐρανὸν καὶ τὴν γῆν καὶ πάντα τὰ ἐν αὐτοῖς καὶ πᾶσιν ἡμῖν

---

¹ ἑξῆς, adv, in the next place

² θεοσεβέω pres act inf, worship God

³ οἴομαι pres mid/pass ind 1s, think, suppose

⁴ μάλιστα, superl, most of all, above all

⁵ ποθέω pres act inf, desire, wish (for)

⁶ τοίνυν, conj, hence, so, well (then)

⁷ ἀπέχω pres mid/pass ind 3p, be paid in full

⁸ προλέγω perf mid/pass ptcp f.s.gen., tell beforehand/in advance

⁹ λατρεία, ας, ἡ, service, worship (of God)

¹⁰ σέβω pres act inf, worship, show reverence/respect for

¹¹ δεσπότης, ου, ὁ, lord, master, owner

¹² ἀξιόω pres act ind 3p, consider worthy

¹³ φρονέω pres act inf, think

¹⁴ προλέγω perf mid/pass ptcp m.p.dat., tell beforehand/in advance

¹⁵ ὁμοιοτρόπως, adv, in the same way

¹⁶ θρησκεία, ας, ἡ, worship

¹⁷ προσάγω pres act ind 3p, bring (forward), come near

¹⁸ διαμαρτάνω pres act ind 3p, miss the mark badly, be quite wrong

¹⁹ ἀναίσθητος, ον, without feeling, perception

²⁰ κωφός, ή, όν, mute, deaf

²¹ Ἕλλην, ηνος, ὁ, Greek, gentile

²² ἀφροσύνη, ης, ἡ, foolishness, lack of sense

²³ δεῖγμα, ατος, τό, indicator, proof, example

²⁴ παρέχω pres act in 3p, give up

²⁵ καθάπερ, conj, just as

²⁶ προσδέομαι pres mid/pass ptcp m.s.dat., need

²⁷ παρέχω pres act inf, give up, offer, present, grant, show

²⁸ μωρία, ας, ἡ, foolishness

²⁹ εἰκός, ότος, το, probable, reasonable

³⁰ ἡγέομαι pres mid/pass opt 3p, lead, guide

³¹ θεοσέβεια, ας, ἡ, piety, godliness

χορηγῶν[1] ὧν προσδεόμεθα,[2] οὐδενὸς ἂν αὐτὸς προσδέοιτο[3] τούτων ὧν τοῖς οἰομένοις[4] διδόναι παρέχει[5] αὐτός. **5** οἱ δέ γε[6] θυσίας[7] αὐτῷ δι᾽ αἵματος καὶ κνίσης[8] καὶ ὁλοκαυτωμάτων[9] ἐπιτελεῖν[10] οἰόμενοι[11] καὶ ταύταις ταῖς τιμαῖς αὐτὸν γεραίρειν,[12] οὐδέν μοι δοκοῦσι διαφέρειν[13] τῶν εἰς τὰ κωφὰ[14] τὴν αὐτὴν ἐνδεικνυμένων[15]φιλοτιμίαν·[16] τῶν μὲν μὴ δυναμένοις τῆς τιμῆς μεταλαμβάνειν,[17] τῶν δὲ δοκούντων παρέχειν[18] τῷ μηδενὸς προσδεομένῳ.[19]

4:1 Ἀλλὰ μὴν[20] τό γε[21] περὶ τὰς βρώσεις[22] αὐτῶν ψοφοδεές,[23] καὶ τὴν περὶ τὰ σάββατα δεισιδαιμονίαν,[24] καὶ τὴν τῆς περιτομῆς ἀλαζονείαν,[25] καὶ τὴν τῆς νηστείας[26] καὶ νουμηνίας[27] εἰρωνείαν,[28]

---

[1] χορηγέω pres act ptcp m.s.nom., provide, supply (in abundance)

[2] προσδέομαι pres mid/pass ind 1p, need

[3] προσδέομαι pres mid/pass opt 3s, need

[4] οἴομαι pres mid/pass ptcp m.p.dat., think, suppose

[5] παρέχω pres act ind 3s, give up, offer, present

[6] γέ, part, at least, even, indeed

[7] θυσία, ας, ἡ, offering, sacrifice

[8] κνῖσα, ης, ἡ, the odor of burning fat

[9] ὁλοκαύτωμα, ατος, τό, whole burnt offering, holocaust

[10] ἐπιτελέω pres act inf, end, complete

[11] οἴομαι pres mid/pass ptcp m.p.nom., think, suppose

[12] γεραίρω pres act inf, honor

[13] διαφέρω pres act inf, carry through, differ, be different

[14] κωφός, ή, όν, mute, deaf

[15] ἐνδείκνυμι pres mid/pass ptcp m.p.gen., show, demonstrate

[16] φιλοτιμία, ας, ἡ, generous zeal

[17] μεταλαμβάνω pres act inf, have a share in, receive

[18] παρέχω pres act inf, give up, offer present

[19] προσδέομαι pres mid/pass ptcp m.s.dat., need

[20] μήν, part, indeed, on the other hand

[21] γέ, part, even, indeed

[22] βρῶσις, εως, ἡ, eating, food

[23] ψοφοδεής, ές, timid, anxious

[24] δεισιδαιμονία, ας, ἡ, religious scruple, religion

[25] ἀλαζονεία, ας, ἡ, pretension, arrogance

[26] νηστεία, ας, ἡ, going hungry, fast

[27] νουμηνία, ας, ἡ, new moon, new moon festival

[28] εἰρωνεία, ας, ἡ, pretense, posturing

καταγέλαστα¹ καὶ οὐδενὸς ἄξια λόγου οὐ νομίζω² σε χρῄζειν³ παρ' ἐμοῦ μαθεῖν.⁴ **2** τό τε γὰρ τῶν ὑπὸ τοῦ Θεοῦ κτισθέντων⁵ εἰς χρῆσιν⁶ ἀνθρώπων ἃ μὲν ὡς καλῶς κτισθέντα⁷ παραδέχεσθαι,⁸ ἃ δ' ὡς ἄχρηστα⁹ καὶ περισσὰ¹⁰ παραιτεῖσθαι,¹¹ πῶς οὐκ ἀθέμιστον;¹² **3** τὸ δὲ καταψεύδεσθαι¹³ Θεοῦ ὡς κωλύοντος¹⁴ ἐν τῇ τῶν σαββάτων ἡμέρᾳ καλόν τι ποιεῖν, πῶς οὐκ ἀσεβές;¹⁵ **4** τὸ δὲ καὶ τὴν μείνωσιν¹⁶ τῆς σαρκὸς μαρτύριον¹⁷ ἐκλογῆς¹⁸ ἀλαζονεύεσθαι¹⁹ ὡς διὰ τοῦτο ἐξαιρέτως²⁰ ἠγαπημένους ὑπὸ Θεοῦ, πῶς οὐ χλεύης²¹ ἄξιον; **5** τὸ δὲ παρεδρεύοντας²² αὐτοὺς ἄστροις²³ καὶ σελήνῃ²⁴ τὴν παρατήρησιν²⁵ τῶν μηνῶν²⁶ καὶ τῶν ἡμερῶν ποιεῖσθαι, καὶ τὰς οἰκονομίας²⁷ Θεοῦ καὶ τὰς τῶν καιρῶν ἀλλαγὰς²⁸ καταδιαιρεῖν²⁹ πρὸς τὰς

---

¹ καταγέλαστος, ον, ridiculous
² νομίζω pres act ind 1s, think, consider
³ χρῄζω pres act inf, (have) need (of)
⁴ μανθάνω aor act inf, learn, appropriate to oneself, hear
⁵ κτίζω aor pass ptcp n.p.gen., create
⁶ χρῆσις, εως, ἡ, use, relations, function
⁷ κτίζω aor pass ptcp n.p.acc., create
⁸ παραδέχομαι pres mid/pass inf, accept, receive
⁹ ἄχρηστος, ον, useless, worthless
¹⁰ περισσός, ή, όν, extraordinary, remarkable
¹¹ παραιτέομαι pres mid/pass inf, ask for, request
¹² ἀθέμιτος, ον, forbidden, unseemly
¹³ καταψεύδω pres mid/pass inf, speak falsely
¹⁴ κωλύω pres act ptcp m.s.gen., hinder, prevent, forbid

¹⁵ ἀσεβής, ές, irreverent, ungodly
¹⁶ μείνωσις, εως, ἡ, diminution, mutilation
¹⁷ μαρτύριον, ου, τό, testimony, proof
¹⁸ ἐκλογή, ῆς, ἡ, selection, choice, election
¹⁹ ἀλαζονεύομαι pres mid/pass inf, boast
²⁰ ἐξαιρέτως, adv, especially
²¹ χλεύη, ης, ἡ, scorn, ridicule
²² παρεδρεύω pres act ptcp m.p.acc., apply oneself to, concern oneself with
²³ ἄστρον, ου, τό, star, constellation
²⁴ σελήνη, ης, ἡ, moon
²⁵ παρατήρησις, εως, ἡ, observation, observance
²⁶ μήν, μηνός, ὁ, month, new moon
²⁷ οἰκονομία, ας, ἡ, management, arrangement
²⁸ ἀλλαγή, ῆς, ἡ, a change
²⁹ καταδιαιρέω pres act inf, divide, make a distinction between

αὐτῶν ὁρμάς,[1] ἃς μὲν εἰς ἑορτάς,[2] ἃς δὲ εἰς πένθη·[3] τίς ἂν θεοσεβείας[4] καὶ οὐκ ἀφροσύνης[5] πολὺ πλέον ἡγήσαιτο[6] δεῖγμα;[7] **6** τῆς μὲν οὖν κοινῆς[8] εἰκαιότητος[9] καὶ ἀπάτης[10] καὶ τῆς Ἰουδαίων πολυπραγμοσύνης[11] καὶ ἀλαζονείας[12] ὡς ὀρθῶς[13] ἀπέχονται[14] Χριστιανοί,[15] ἀρκούντως[16] σε νομίζω[17] μεμαθηκέναι·[18] τὸ δὲ τῆς ἰδίας αὐτῶν θεοσεβείας[19] μυστήριον[20] μὴ προσδοκήσῃς[21] δύνασθαι παρὰ ἀνθρώπου μαθεῖν.[22]

5:1 Χριστιανοὶ[23] γὰρ οὔτε γῇ οὔτε φωνῇ οὔτε ἔσθεσι[24] διακεκριμένοι[25] τῶν λοιπῶν εἰσιν ἀνθρώπων. **2** οὔτε γάρ που[26] πόλεις ἰδίας κατοικοῦσιν οὔτε διαλέκτῳ[27] τινὶ παρηλλαγμένῃ[28]

---

[1] ὁρμή, ῆς, ἡ, impulse, inclination, desire

[2] ἑορτή, ῆς, ἡ, festival, celebration

[3] πένθος, ους, τό, grief, sadness, mourning

[4] θεοσέβεια, ας, ἡ, piety, godliness

[5] ἀφροσύνη, ης, ἡ, foolishness, lack of sense

[6] ἡγέομαι aor mid opt 3s, lead, guide

[7] δεῖγμα, ατος, τό, indicator, proof, example

[8] κοινός, ή, όν, communal, ordinary, profane

[9] εἰκαιότης, ητος, ἡ, silliness

[10] ἀπάτη, ης, ἡ, deception, deceitfulness, pleasure, pleasantness

[11] πολυπραγμοσύνη, ης, ἡ, fussiness

[12] ἀλαζονεία, ας, ἡ, pretension, arrogance

[13] ὀρθῶς, adv, rightly, correctly

[14] ἀπέχω pres mid/pass ind 3p, be paid/receive in full

[15] Χριστιανός, οῦ, ὁ, Christ-partisan, Christian

[16] ἀρκούντως, adv, sufficiently

[17] νομίζω pres act ind 1s, think, consider

[18] μανθάνω perf act inf, learn

[19] θεοσέβεια, ας, ἡ, piety, godliness

[20] μυστήριον, ου, τό, (God's) secret, transcendent/ultimate reality

[21] προσδοκάω aor act sub, wait for, look for

[22] μανθάνω aor act inf, learn

[23] Χριστιανός, οῦ, ὁ, Christ-partisan, Christian

[24] ἐσθής, ῆτος, ἡ, clothing

[25] διακρίνω perf mid/pass ptcp m.p.nom., separate

[26] πού, part, where

[27] διάλεκτος, ου, ἡ, language

[28] παραλλάσσω perf mid/pass ptcp f.s.dat., change

χρῶνται[1] οὔτε βίον[2] παράσημον[3] ἀσκοῦσιν.[4] **3** οὐ μὴν[5] ἐπινοίᾳ[6] τινὶ καὶ φροντίδι[7] πολυπραγμόνων[8] ἀνθρώπων μάθημα[9] τοιοῦτ' αὐτοῖς ἐστιν εὑρημένον, οὐδὲ δόγματος[10] ἀνθρωπίνου[11] προεστᾶσιν[12] ὥσπερ ἔνιοι.[13] **4** κατοικοῦντες δὲ πόλεις Ἑλληνίδας[14] τε καὶ βαρβάρους[15] ὡς ἕκαστος ἐκληρώθη,[16] καὶ τοῖς ἐγχωρίοις[17] ἔθεσιν[18] ἀκολουθοῦντες ἔν τε ἐσθῆτι[19] καὶ διαίτῃ[20] καὶ τῷ λοιπῷ βίῳ,[21] θαυμαστὴν[22] καὶ ὁμολογουμένως[23] παράδοξον[24] ἐνδείκνυνται[25] τὴν κατάστασιν τῆς ἑαυτῶν πολιτείας.[26] **5** πατρίδας[27] οἰκοῦσιν[28] ἰδίας, ἀλλ' ὡς πάροικοι·[29] μετέχουσι[30] πάντων ὡς πολῖται,[31] καὶ πάνθ' ὑπομένουσιν[32] ὡς

---

[1] χράομαι pres mid/pass ind 3p, make use of, employ
[2] βίος, ου, ὁ, life, means of subsistence
[3] παράσημος, ον, peculiar, odd
[4] ἀσκέω pres act ind 3p, practice, engage in
[5] μήν, part, indeed, on the other hand
[6] ἐπίνοια, ας, ἡ, thought, conception
[7] φροντίς, ίδος, ἡ, reflection, thought
[8] πολυπράγμων, ον, inquisitive
[9] μάθημα, ατος, τό, knowledge, teaching
[10] δόγμα, ατος, τό, ordinance, decision
[11] ἀνθρώπινος, η, ον, human
[12] προΐστημι aor act ind 3p, rule
[13] ἔνιοι, αι, α, some, several
[14] Ἑλληνίς, ίδος, ἡ, Greek
[15] βάρβαρος, ον, foreign-speaking, non-Hellenic, foreigner
[16] κληρόω aor pass ind 3s, appoint by lot, obtain by lot

[17] ἐγχώριος, ον, local
[18] ἔθος, ους, τό, habit, custom
[19] ἐσθής, ῆτος, ἡ, clothing
[20] δίαιτα, ης, ἡ, food, diet
[21] βίος, ου, ὁ, life
[22] θαυμαστός, ή, όν, wonderful, marvelous
[23] ὁμολογουμένως, adv, incontestable, undeniably
[24] παράδοξος, ον, strange, wonderful
[25] ἐνδείκνυμι pres mid/pass ind 3p, show, demonstrate
[26] πολιτεία, ας, ἡ, state
[27] πατρίς, ίδος, ἡ, fatherland, homeland
[28] οἰκέω pres act ind 3p, live, dwell
[29] πάροικος, ον, strange, stranger
[30] μετέχω pres act ind 3p, share, participate
[31] πολίτης, ου, ὁ, citizen, fellow-citizen
[32] ὑπομένω pres act ind 3p, remain/stay (behind), endure

ξένοι·[1] πᾶσα ξένη[2] πατρίς[3] ἐστιν αὐτῶν, καὶ πᾶσα πατρὶς[4] ξένη.[5] **6** γαμοῦσιν[6] ὡς πάντες, τεκνογονοῦσιν·[7] ἀλλ' οὐ ῥίπτουσι[8] τὰ γεννώμενα. **7** τράπεζαν[9] κοινὴν[10] παρατίθενται,[11] ἀλλ' οὐ κοιτήν.[12] **8** ἐν σαρκὶ τυγχάνουσιν,[13] ἀλλ' οὐ κατὰ σάρκα ζῶσιν. **9** ἐπὶ γῆς διατρίβουσιν,[14] ἀλλ' ἐν οὐρανῷ πολιτεύονται.[15] **10** πείθονται τοῖς ὡρισμένοις[16] νόμοις, καὶ τοῖς ἰδίοις βίοις[17] νικῶσι[18] τοὺς νόμους. **11** ἀγαπῶσι πάντας, καὶ ὑπὸ πάντων διώκονται. **12** ἀγνοοῦνται,[19] καὶ κατακρίνονται·[20] θανατοῦνται,[21] καὶ ζωοποιοῦνται.[22] **13** πτωχεύουσι,[23] καὶ πλου-τίζουσι[24] πολλούς· πάντων ὑστεροῦνται,[25] καὶ ἐν πᾶσι περισσεύουσιν. **14** ἀτιμοῦνται,[26] καὶ ἐν ταῖς ἀτιμίαις[27] δοξ-άζονται· βλασφημοῦνται, καὶ δικαιοῦνται. **15** λοιδοροῦνται,[28]

---

[1] ξένος, η, ον, strange, stranger

[2] ξένος, η, ον, strange, stranger

[3] πατρίς, ίδος, ἡ, fatherland, homeland

[4] πατρίς, ίδος, ἡ, fatherland, homeland

[5] ξένος, η, ον, strange, stranger

[6] γαμέω pres act ind 3p, marry

[7] τεκνογονέω pres act ind 3p, bear/beget children

[8] ῥίπτω pres act ind 3p, throw, put/lay down

[9] τράπεζα, ης, ἡ, table, meal, food

[10] κοινός, ή, όν, common, ordinary

[11] παρατίθημι pres mid/pass ind 3p, set/put before, demonstrate

[12] κοίτη, ης, ἡ, bed, marriage-bed

[13] τυγχάνω pres act ind 3p, meet, attain, find

[14] διατρίβω pres act in 3p, spend time

[15] πολιτεύομαι pres mid/pass ind 3p, have one's citizenship/home

[16] ὁρίζω perf mid/pass ptcp m.p.dat., set limits to, define

[17] βιός, οῦ, ὁ, life

[18] νικάω pres act. ind 3p, conquer, overcome, excel

[19] ἀγνοέω pres mid/pass ind 3p, not to know

[20] κατακρίνω pres mid/pass ind 3p, pronounce a sentence on

[21] θανατόω pres mid/pass ind 3p, put to death, bring death

[22] ζωοποιέω pres mid/pass ind 3p, make alive, give life to

[23] πτωχεύω pres act ind 3p, be poor

[24] πλουτίζω pres act ind 3p, make wealthy, make rich

[25] ὑστερέω pres mid/pass ind 3p, miss

[26] ἀτιμόω pres mid/pass ind 3p, dishonor

[27] ἀτιμία, ας, ἡ, dishonor

[28] λοιδορέω pres mid/pass ind 3p, revile, abuse

καὶ εὐλογοῦσιν· ὑβρίζονται,[1] καὶ τιμῶσιν.[2] **16** ἀγαθοποιοῦντες[3] ὡς κακοὶ κολάζονται·[4] κολαζόμενοι[5] χαίρουσιν ὡς ζωοποιούμενοι.[6] **17** ὑπὸ Ἰουδαίων ὡς ἀλλόφυλοι[7] πολεμοῦνται,[8] καὶ ὑπὸ Ἑλλήνων[9] διώκονται, καὶ τὴν αἰτίαν[10] τῆς ἔχθρας[11] εἰπεῖν οἱ μισοῦντες οὐκ ἔχουσιν.

6:1 Ἁπλῶς[12] δ᾽ εἰπεῖν, ὅπερ[13] ἐστὶν ἐν σώματι ψυχή, τοῦτ᾽ εἰσὶν ἐν κόσμῳ Χριστιανοί.[14] **2** ἔσπαρται κατὰ πάντων τῶν τοῦ σώματος μελῶν ἡ ψυχή, καὶ Χριστιανοὶ[15] κατὰ τὰς τοῦ κόσμου πόλεις. **3** οἰκεῖ[16] μὲν ἐν τῷ σώματι ψυχή, οὐκ ἔστι δὲ ἐκ τοῦ σώματος· καὶ Χριστιανοὶ[17] ἐν κόσμῳ οἰκοῦσιν,[18] οὐκ εἰσὶ δὲ ἐκ τοῦ κόσμου. **4** ἀόρατος[19] ἡ ψυχὴ ἐν ὁρατῷ[20] φρουρεῖται[21] τῷ σώματι· καὶ Χριστιανοὶ[22] γινώσκονται μὲν ὄντες ἐν τῷ κόσμῳ, ἀόρατος[23] δὲ αὐτῶν ἡ θεοσέβεια[24] μένει. **5** μισεῖ τὴν ψυχὴν ἡ σὰρξ

---

[1] ὑβρίζω pres mid/pass ind 3p, mistreat, scoff at, insult

[2] τιμάω pres act ind 3p, estimate, value

[3] ἀγαθοποιέω pres act ptcp m.p.nom., do good

[4] κολάζω pres mid/pass ind 3p, penalize, punish

[5] κολάζω pres mid/pass ptcp m.p.nom., penalize punish

[6] ζωοποιέω pres mid/pass ptcp m.p. nom., make alive, give life to

[7] ἀλλόφυλος, ον, alien, foreign

[8] πολεμέω pres mid/pass ind 3p, wage war, be hostile

[9] Ἕλλην, ηνος, ὁ, Greek, gentile

[10] αἰτία, ας, ἡ, cause, reason

[11] ἔχθρα, ας, ἡ, enmity

[12] ἁπλῶς, adv, simply, sincerely

[13] ὅσπερ, ἥ, ὅ, who indeed, which indeed

[14] Χριστιανός, οῦ, ὁ, Christ-partisan, Christian

[15] Χριστιανός, οῦ, ὁ, Christ-partisan, Christian

[16] οἰκέω pres act ind 3s, live, dwell

[17] Χριστιανός, οῦ, ὁ, Christ-partisan, Christian

[18] οἰκέω pres act ind 3p, live, dwell

[19] ἀόρατος, ον, unseen, invisible

[20] ὁρατός, ή, όν, visible

[21] φρουρέω pres mid/pass ind 3s, guard, detain

[22] Χριστιανός, οῦ, ὁ, Christ-partisan, Christian

[23] ἀόρατος, ον, unseen, invisible

[24] θεοσέβεια, ας, ἡ, piety, godliness

καὶ πολεμεῖ[1] μηδὲν ἀδικουμένη,[2] διότι[3] ταῖς ἡδοναῖς[4] κωλύεται[5] χρῆσθαι.[6] μισεῖ καὶ Χριστιανοὺς[7] ὁ κόσμος μηδὲν ἀδικούμενος,[8] ὅτι ταῖς ἡδοναῖς[9] ἀντιτάσσονται.[10] **6** ἡ ψυχὴ τὴν μισοῦσαν ἀγαπᾷ σάρκα καὶ τὰ μέλη· καὶ Χριστιανοὶ[11] τοὺς μισοῦντας ἀγαπῶσιν. **7** ἐγκέκλεισται[12] μὲν ἡ ψυχὴ τῷ σώματι, συνέχει[13] δὲ αὐτὴ τὸ σῶμα· καὶ Χριστιανοὶ[14] κατέχονται[15] μὲν ὡς ἐν φρουρᾷ[16] τῷ κόσμῳ, αὐτοὶ δὲ συνέχουσι[17] τὸν κόσμον. **8** ἀθάνατος[18] ἡ ψυχὴ ἐν θνητῷ[19] σκηνώματι[20] κατοικεῖ· καὶ Χριστιανοὶ[21] παροικοῦσιν[22] ἐν φθαρτοῖς, τὴν ἐν οὐρανοῖς[23] ἀφθαρσίαν[24] προσδεχόμενοι.[25] **9** κακουργουμένη[26] σιτίοις[27] καὶ ποτοῖς[28] ἡ ψυχὴ βελτιοῦται·[29] καὶ Χριστιανοὶ[30] κολαζόμενοι[31] καθ'

---

[1] πολεμέω pres act ind 3s, wage war, be hostile

[2] ἀδικέω pres mid/pass ptcp f.s.nom., do wrong, injure

[3] διότι, conj, because, therefore, that

[4] ἡδονή, ῆς, ἡ, delight, enjoyment

[5] κωλύω pres mid/pass ind 3s, prevent, forbid

[6] χράομαι pres mid/pass inf, make use of

[7] Χριστιανός, οῦ, ὁ, Christ-partisan, Christian

[8] ἀδικέω pres mid/pass ptcp m.s.nom., do wrong, injure

[9] ἡδονή, ῆς, ἡ, delight, enjoyment

[10] ἀντιτάσσω pres mid/pass ind 3p, oppose, resist

[11] Χριστιανός, οῦ, ὁ, Christ-partisan, Christian

[12] ἐγκλείω perf mid/pass ind 3s, lock up, shut up, enclose

[13] συνέχω pres act ind 3s, hold together, sustain

[14] Χριστιανός, οῦ, ὁ, Christ-partisan, Christian

[15] κατέχω pres mid/pass ind 3p, prevent, hinder

[16] φρουρά, ᾶς, ἡ, guard-duty, service as sentinel, prison

[17] συνέχω pres act ind 3p, hold together, sustain

[18] ἀθάνατος, ον, immortal

[19] θνητός, ή, όν, mortal

[20] σκήνωμα, ατος, τό, habitation

[21] Χριστιανός, οῦ, ὁ, Christ-partisan, Christian

[22] παροικέω pres act ind 3p, live nearby, dwell beside

[23] φθαρτός, ή, όν, perishable

[24] ἀφθαρσία, ας, ἡ, incorruptibility, immortality

[25] προσδέχομαι pres mid/pass ptcp m.p.nom., take up, receive, welcome, wait for

[26] κακουργέω pres mid/pass ptcp f.s.nom., treat badly

[27] σιτίον, ου, τό, food

[28] ποτόν, οῦ, τό, drink

[29] βελτιόω pres mid/pass ind 3s, improve, become better

[30] Χριστιανός, οῦ, ὁ, Christ-partisan, Christian

[31] κολάζω pres mid/pass ptcp m.p.nom., penalize, punish

ἡμέραν πλεονάζουσι[1] μᾶλλον. **10** εἰς τοσαύτην[2] αὐτοὺς τάξιν[3] ἔθετο ὁ Θεός, ἣν οὐ θεμιτὸν[4] αὐτοῖς παραιτήσασθαι.[5]

7:1 Οὐ γὰρ ἐπίγειον,[6] ὡς ἔφην, εὕρημα[7] τοῦτ᾽ αὐτοῖς παρεδόθη, οὐδὲ θνητὴν[8] ἐπίνοιαν[9] φυλάσσειν οὕτως ἀξιοῦσιν[10] ἐπιμελῶς,[11] οὐδὲ ἀνθρωπίνων[12] οἰκονομίαν[13] μυστηρίων[14] πεπίστευνται. **2** ἀλλ᾽ αὐτὸς ἀληθῶς[15] ὁ παντοκράτωρ[16] καὶ παντοκτίστης[17] καὶ ἀόρατος[18] Θεός, αὐτὸς ἀπ᾽ οὐρανῶν τὴν ἀλήθειαν καὶ τὸν λόγον τὸν ἅγιον καὶ ἀπερινόητον[19] ἀνθρώποις ἐνίδρυσε[20] καὶ ἐγκατεστήριξε[21] ταῖς καρδίαις αὐτῶν, οὐ καθάπερ[22] ἄν τις εἰκάσειεν[23] ἄνθρωπος ὑπηρέτην[24] τινὰ πέμψας ἢ ἄγγελον ἢ ἄρχοντα ἢ τινα τῶν διεπόντων[25] τὰ ἐπίγεια[26] ἢ τινα τῶν

---

[1] πλεονάζω pres act ind 3p, be/become more, increase
[2] τοσοῦτος, αύτη, οῦτον, so many, so much
[3] τάξις, εως, ἡ, fixed succession, order
[4] θεμιτός, ή, όν, allowed, permitted, right
[5] παραιτέομαι aor mid inf, ask for, request
[6] ἐπίγειος, ον, earthly, worldly things
[7] εὕρημα, ατος, τό, discovery, invention
[8] θνητός, ή, όν, mortal
[9] ἐπίνοια, ας, ἡ, thought, conception
[10] ἀξιόω pres act ind 3p, consider worthy
[11] ἐπιμελῶς, adv, carefully, diligently
[12] ἀνθρώπινος, η, ον, human
[13] οἰκονομία, ας, ἡ, management, arrangement
[14] μυστήριον, ου, τό, (God's) secret, transcendent/ultimate reality, secret
[15] ἀληθῶς, adv, truly, actually
[16] παντοκράτωρ, ορος, ὁ, Almighty, All-powerful
[17] παντοκτίστης, ου, ἡ, creator of the universe
[18] ἀόρατος, ον, unseen, invisible
[19] ἀπερινόητος, ον, incomprehensible
[20] ἐνιδρύω aor act ind 3s, place/establish in
[21] ἐγκαταστηρίζω aor act ind 3s, establish
[22] καθάπερ, conj, just as
[23] εἰκάζω aor act opt 3s, suppose, imagine
[24] ὑπηρέτης, ου, ὁ, helper, assistant
[25] διέπω pres act ptcp m.p.gen., conduct, administer
[26] ἐπίγειος, ον, earthly, worldly things

πεπιστευμένων τὰς ἐν οὐρανοῖς διοικήσεις,[1] ἀλλ' αὐτὸν τὸν τεχνίτην[2] καὶ δημιουργὸν[3] τῶν ὅλων, ᾧ τοὺς οὐρανοὺς ἔκτισεν,[4] ᾧ τὴν θάλασσαν ἰδίοις ὅροις[5] ἐνέκλεισεν,[6] οὗ τὰ μυστήρια[7] πιστῶς[8] πάντα φυλάσσει τὰ στοιχεῖα,[9] παρ' οὗ τὰ μέτρα[10] τῶν τῆς ἡμέρας δρόμων[11] ἥλιος εἴληφε φυλάσσειν, ᾧ πειθαρχεῖ[12] σελήνη[13] νυκτὶ φαίνειν κελεύοντι,[14] ᾧ πειθαρχεῖ[15] τὰ ἄστρα[16] τῷ τῆς σελήνης[17] ἀκολουθοῦντα δρόμῳ,[18] ᾧ πάντα διατέτακται[19] καὶ διώρισται[20] καὶ ὑποτέτακται, οὐρανοὶ καὶ τὰ ἐν οὐρανοῖς, γῆ καὶ τὰ ἐν τῇ γῇ, θάλασσα καὶ τὰ ἐν τῇ θαλάσσῃ, πῦρ, ἀήρ,[21] ἄβυσσος,[22] τὰ ἐν ὕψεσι,[23] τὰ ἐν βάθεσι,[24] τὰ ἐν τῷ μεταξύ·[25] τοῦτον πρὸς αὐτοὺς ἀπέστειλεν. **3** ἆρά[26] γε,[27] ὡς ἀνθρώπων ἄν τις λογίσαιτο, ἐπὶ τυραννίδι[28] καὶ φόβῳ καὶ καταπλήξει;[29] **4** οὐμενοῦν· ἀλλ' ἐν ἐπιεικείᾳ[30] καὶ πραΰτητι[31] ὡς βασιλεὺς

---

[1] διοίκησις, εως, ἡ, administration, management

[2] τεχνίτης, ου, ὁ, craftsperson, artisan, designer

[3] δημιουργός, οῦ, ὁ, builder, maker, creator

[4] κτίζω aor act ind 3s, create

[5] ὄρος, ους, τό, mountain, mount, hill

[6] ἐγκλείω aor act ind 3s, lock up, shut up

[7] μυστήριον, ου, τό, (God's) secret, transcendent/ultimate reality

[8] πιστῶς, adv, faithfully

[9] στοιχεῖον, ου, τό, elements, heavenly bodies, fundamental principles

[10] μέτρον, ου, τό, measure, quantity

[11] δρόμος, ου, ὁ, course, course of life

[12] πειθαρχέω pres act ind 3s, obey

[13] σελήνη, ης, ἡ, moon

[14] κελεύω pres act ptcp m.s.dat., command, order, urge

[15] πειθαρχέω pres act ind 3s, obey

[16] ἄστρον, ου, τό, star, constellation

[17] σελήνη, ης, ἡ, moon

[18] δρόμος, ου, ὁ, course, course of life, mission

[19] διατάσσω perf mid/pass ind 3s, make arrangements, order

[20] διορίζω perf mid/pass ind 3s, set limits to

[21] ἀήρ, έρος, ὁ, air, sky, space

[22] ἄβυσσος, ου, ἡ, depth, abyss, netherworld

[23] ὕψος, ους, τό, height, pride

[24] βάθος, ους, τό, depth

[25] μεταξύ, adv, between, next

[26] ἆρα, conj, so, then

[27] γέ, part, at least, even

[28] τυραννίς, ίδος, ἡ, despotic rule, tyranny

[29] καταπλήσσω fut act ind 3s, amaze, astound

[30] ἐπιείκεια, ας, ἡ, clemency, gentleness

[31] πραΰτης, ητος, ἡ, gentleness, humility

πέμπων υἱὸν βασιλέα ἔπεμψεν, ὡς Θεὸν ἔπεμψεν, ὡς ἄνθρωπον πρὸς ἀνθρώπους ἔπεμψεν, ὡς σώζων ἔπεμψεν, ὡς πείθων, οὐ βιαζόμενος·[1] βία[2] γὰρ οὐ πρόσεστι[3] τῷ Θεῷ. **5** ἔπεμψεν ὡς καλῶν, οὐ διώκων· ἔπεμψεν ὡς ἀγαπῶν, οὐ κρίνων. **6** πέμψει γὰρ αὐτὸν κρίνοντα, καὶ τίς αὐτοῦ τὴν παρουσίαν[4] ὑποστήσεται;[5] **7** Οὐχ ὁρᾷς παραβαλλομένους[6] θηρίοις, ἵνα ἀρνήσωνται τὸν Κύριον, καὶ μὴ νικωμένους;[7] **8** οὐχ ὁρᾷς ὅσῳ πλείονες κολάζονται,[8] τοσούτῳ[9] πλεονάζοντας[10] ἄλλους; **9** ταῦτα ἀνθρώπου οὐ δοκεῖ τὰ ἔργα, ταῦτα δύναμίς ἐστι Θεοῦ· ταῦτα τῆς παρουσίας[11] αὐτοῦ δείγματα.[12]

8:1 Τίς γὰρ ὅλως[13] ἀνθρώπων ἠπίστατο[14] τί ποτ᾽[15] ἐστὶ Θεός, πρὶν[16] αὐτὸν ἐλθεῖν; **2** ἢ τοὺς κενοὺς[17] καὶ ληρώδεις[18] ἐκείνων λόγους ἀποδέχῃ[19] τῶν ἀξιοπίστων[20] φιλοσόφων;[21] ὧν οἱ μέν τινες πῦρ ἔφασαν εἶναι τὸν θεόν (οὗ μέλλουσι χωρήσειν[22] αὐτοί, τοῦτο καλοῦσι θεόν) οἱ δὲ ὕδωρ, οἱ δ᾽ ἄλλο τι τῶν στοιχείων[23] τῶν

---

[1] βιάζω pres mid/pass ptcp m.s.nom., dominate, constrain
[2] βία, ας, ἡ, force
[3] πρόσειμι pres act ind 3s, belong to, be present with
[4] παρουσία, ας, ἡ, presence, coming
[5] ὑφίστημι fut mid ind 3s, resist, face, endure
[6] παραβάλλω pres mid/pass ptcp m.p.acc., throw to, give up
[7] νικάω pres mid/pass ptcp m.p.acc., conquer, prevail
[8] κολάζω pres mid/pass ind 3p, penalize, punish
[9] τοσοῦτος, αύτη, οῦτον, so many, so much
[10] πλεονάζω pres act ptcp m.p.acc., be/become more, increase
[11] παρουσία, ας, ἡ, presence, coming

[12] δεῖγμα, ατος, τό, indicator, proof
[13] ὅλως, adv, completely, wholly
[14] ἐπίσταμαι imp mid/pass ind 3s, understand, know
[15] ποτέ, conj, at some time or other
[16] πρίν, conj/adv, before
[17] κενός, ή, όν, empty, in vain
[18] ληρώδης, ες, foolish, silly, frivolous
[19] ἀποδέχομαι pres mid/pass ind 2s, welcome, acknowledge
[20] ἀξιόπιστος, ον, trustworthy, pretentiousness
[21] φιλόσοφος, ου, ὁ, philosopher
[22] χωρέω fut act inf, go, go out/away, reach
[23] στοιχεῖον, ου, τό, elements, heavenly bodies, fundamental principles

ἐκτισμένων[1] ὑπὸ Θεοῦ. **3** καίτοι[2] γε[3] εἴ τις τούτων τῶν λόγων ἀπόδεκτός[4] ἐστι, δύναιτ᾽ ἂν καὶ τῶν λοιπῶν κτισμάτων[5] ἓν ἕκαστον ὁμοίως ἀποφαίνεσθαι[6] Θεόν. **4** ἀλλὰ ταῦτα μὲν τερατεία[7] καὶ τερατεία[8] τῶν γοήτων[9] ἐστίν. **5** ἀνθρώπων δὲ οὐδεὶς οὔτε εἶδεν οὔτε ἐγνώρισεν,[10] αὐτὸς δὲ ἑαυτὸν ἐπέδειξεν.[11] **6** ἐπέδειξε[12] δὲ διὰ πίστεως, ᾗ μόνῃ Θεὸν ἰδεῖν συγκεχώρηται.[13] **7** ὁ γὰρ δεσπότης[14] καὶ δημιουργὸς[15] τῶν ὅλων Θεός, ὁ ποιήσας τὰ πάντα καὶ κατὰ τάξιν[16] διακρίνας,[17] οὐ μόνον φιλάνθρωπος[18] ἐγένετο ἀλλὰ καὶ μακρόθυμος.[19] **8** ἀλλ᾽ οὗτος ἦν μὲν ἀεὶ[20] τοιοῦτος, καὶ ἔστι, καὶ ἔσται· χρηστὸς[21] καὶ ἀγαθὸς καὶ ἀόργητος[22] καὶ ἀληθής,[23] καὶ μόνος ἀγαθός ἐστιν. **9** ἐννοήσας[24] δὲ μεγάλην καὶ ἄφραστον[25] ἔννοιαν[26] ἀνεκοινώσατο[27] μόνῳ τῷ παιδί.[28]

---

[1] κτίζω perf mid/pass ptcp n.p.gen., create

[2] καίτοι, conj, yet, on the other hand

[3] γέ, part, at least, even

[4] ἀπόδεκτος, ον, acceptable, welcome

[5] κτίσμα, ατος, τό, that which is created, creature

[6] ἀποφαίνω pres mid/pass inf, show forth, display

[7] τερατεία, ας, ἡ, illusion, trickery

[8] τερατεία, ας, ἡ, illusion, trickery

[9] γόης, ητος, ὁ, swindler, cheat

[10] γνωρίζω aor act ind 3s, make known, reveal

[11] ἐπιδείκνυμι aor act ind 3s, show, point out

[12] ἐπιδείκνυμι aor act ind 3s, show, point out

[13] συγχωρέω perf mid/pass ind 3s, grant a little ground, grant

[14] δεσπότης, ου, ὁ, lord, master, owner

[15] δημιουργός, οῦ, ὁ, crafts worker, builder

[16] τάξις, εως, ἡ, fixed succession/order

[17] διακρίνω aor act ptcp m.s.nom., separate, arrange

[18] φιλάνθρωπος, ον, loving humanity, benevolent

[19] μακρόθυμος, ον, patient, forbearing

[20] ἀεί, adv, always, continually

[21] χρηστός, ή, όν, easy, fine, reputable

[22] ἀόργητος, ον, free from anger

[23] ἀληθής, ές, truthful, honest

[24] ἐννοέω aor act ptcp m.s.nom., have in mind, consider

[25] ἄφραστος, ον, too wonderful for words

[26] ἔννοια, ας, ἡ, thought, knowledge

[27] ἀνακοινόω aor mid ind 3s, communicate (something) to someone

[28] παῖς, παιδός, ὁ/ἡ, child, servant

10 ἐν ὅσῳ μὲν οὖν κατεῖχεν[1] ἐν μυστηρίῳ[2] καὶ διετήρει[3] τὴν σοφὴν[4] αὐτοῦ βουλήν,[5] ἀμελεῖν[6] ἡμῶν καὶ ἀφροντιστεῖν[7] ἐδόκει· **11** ἐπεὶ[8] δὲ ἀπεκάλυψε[9] διὰ τοῦ ἀγαπητοῦ παιδὸς[10] καὶ ἐφανέρωσε τὰ ἐξ ἀρχῆς ἡτοιμασμένα, πάνθ' ἅμα[11] παρέσχεν[12] ἡμῖν, καὶ μετασχεῖν[13] τῶν εὐεργεσιῶν[14] αὐτοῦ καὶ ἰδεῖν καὶ νοῆσαι,[15] ἃ τίς ἂν πώποτε[16] προσεδόκησεν[17] ἡμῶν;

9:1 Πάντ' οὖν ἤδη παρ' ἑαυτῷ σὺν τῷ παιδὶ[18] οἰκονομηκώς,[19] μέχρι[20] μὲν τοῦ πρόσθεν[21] χρόνου εἴασεν[22] ἡμᾶς ὡς ἐβουλόμεθα ἀτάκτοις[23] φοραῖς[24] φέρεσθαι, ἡδοναῖς[25] καὶ ἐπιθυμίαις ἀπαγομένους,[26] οὐ πάντως[27] ἐφηδόμενος[28] τοῖς ἁμαρτήμασιν[29]

---

[1] κατέχω imp act ind 3s, prevent, hinder, restrain

[2] μυστήριον, ου, τό, (God's) secret, ultimate/transcendent reality

[3] διατηρέω imp act ind 3s, keep, keep free of

[4] σοφός, ή, όν, clever, skillful, experienced, wise

[5] βουλή, ῆς, ἡ, plan, purpose, intention

[6] ἀμελέω pres act inf, neglect

[7] ἀφροντιστέω pres act inf, be careless, unconcerned

[8] ἐπεί, conj, when, because, since

[9] ἀποκαλύπτω aor act ind 3s, reveal, disclose, bring to light

[10] παῖς, παιδός, ὁ/ἡ, child, servant

[11] ἅμα, impr prep, at the same time, together

[12] παρέχω aor act ind 3s, give up, offer, grant

[13] μετέχω aor act inf, share, participate

[14] εὐεργεσία, ας, ἡ, doing of good, service

[15] νοέω aor act inf, perceive, apprehend

[16] πώποτε, adv, ever, at any time

[17] προσδοκάω aor act ind 3s, wait for, look for

[18] παῖς, παιδός, ὁ/ἡ, child, servant

[19] οἰκονομέω perf act ptcp m.s.nom., administer, manage

[20] μέχρι, impr prep, as far as, until

[21] πρόσθεν, adv, earlier, former

[22] ἐάω aor act ind 3s, let, permit

[23] ἄτακτος, ον, disorderly, insubordinate

[24] φορά, ᾶς, ἡ, impulse, passion

[25] ἡδονή, ῆς, ἡ, pleasure, delight, enjoyment

[26] ἀπάγω pres mid/pass ptcp m.p.acc., lead off, take away

[27] πάντως, adv, by all means, certainly

[28] ἐφήδομαι pres mid/pass ptcp m.s.nom., (take) delight in

[29] ἁμάρτημα, τος, τό, sin, transgression

ἡμῶν, ἀλλ' ἀνεχόμενος,[1] οὐδὲ τῷ τότε τῆς ἀδικίας[2] καιρῷ συνευδοκῶν,[3] ἀλλὰ τὸν νῦν τῆς δικαιοσύνης δημιουργῶν,[4] ἵνα ἐν τῷ τότε χρόνῳ ἐλεγχθέντες[5] ἐκ τῶν ἰδίων ἔργων ἀνάξιοι[6] ζωῆς νῦν ὑπὸ τῆς τοῦ Θεοῦ χρηστότητος[7] ἀξιωθῶμεν,[8] καὶ τὸ καθ' ἑαυτοὺς φανερώσαντες ἀδύνατον[9] εἰσελθεῖν εἰς τὴν βασιλείαν τοῦ Θεοῦ τῇ δυνάμει τοῦ Θεοῦ δυνατοὶ γενηθῶμεν. 2 ἐπεὶ[10] δὲ πεπλήρωτο μὲν ἡ ἡμετέρα[11] ἀδικία,[12] καὶ τελείως[13] πεφανέρωτο ὅτι ὁ μισθὸς[14] αὐτῆς κόλασις[15] καὶ θάνατος προσεδοκᾶτο,[16] ἦλθε δὲ ὁ καιρὸς ὃν Θεὸς προέθετο[17] λοιπὸν φανερῶσαι τὴν ἑαυτοῦ χρηστότητα[18] καὶ δύναμιν (ὢ[19] τῆς ὑπερβαλλούσης[20] φιλανθρωπίας[21] καὶ ἀγάπης τοῦ Θεοῦ), οὐκ ἐμίσησεν ἡμᾶς οὐδὲ ἀπώσατο[22] οὐδὲ ἐμνησικάκησεν,[23] ἀλλὰ ἐμακροθύμησεν,[24] ἠνέσχετο,[25] ἐλεῶν[26] αὐτὸς τὰς ἡμετέρας[27]

---

[1] ἀνέχομαι pres mid/pass ptcp m.s.nom., endure, bear with

[2] ἀδικία, ας, ἡ, wrongdoing, unrighteousness

[3] συνευδοκέω pres act ptcp m.s.nom., agree with, approve of

[4] δημιουργέω pres act ptcp m.s.nom., create

[5] ἐλέγχω aor pass ptcp m.p.nom., bring to light, expose, set forth

[6] ἀνάξιος, ον, unworthy

[7] χρηστότης, ητος, ἡ, uprightness, goodness

[8] ἀξιόω aor pass sub 1p, consider worthy, deserving

[9] ἀδύνατος, ον, powerless, impotent

[10] ἐπεί, conj, when, after, because

[11] ἡμέτερος, α, ον, our

[12] ἀδικία, ας, ἡ, wrongdoing, unrighteousness

[13] τελείως, adv, perfectly, completely

[14] μισθός, οῦ, ὁ, pay, wages, recompense

[15] κόλασις, εως, ἡ, punishment

[16] προσδοκάω imp mid/pass ind 3s, wait for, look for

[17] προστίθημι aor mid ind 3s, add, put to, provide

[18] χρηστότης, ητος, ἡ, uprightness, goodness

[19] ὤ, interj, O, How!

[20] ὑπερβάλλω pres act ptcp f.s.gen., go beyond, surpass, outdo

[21] φιλανθρωπία, ας, ἡ, (loving) kindness

[22] ἀπωθέω aor mid ind 3s, push aside, reject, repudiate

[23] μνησικακέω aor act ind 3s, remember evil

[24] μακροθυμέω aor act ind 3s, have patience

[25] ἀνέχω aor mid ind 3s, endure, bear with

[26] ἐλεέω pres act ptcp m.s.nom., have compassion/mercy/pity

[27] ἡμέτερος, α, ον, our

ἁμαρτίας ἀνεδέξατο,[1] αὐτὸς τὸν ἴδιον υἱὸν ἀπέδοτο λύτρον[2] ὑπὲρ ἡμῶν, τὸν ἅγιον ὑπὲρ ἀνόμων,[3] τὸν ἄκακον[4] ὑπὲρ τῶν κακῶν, τὸν δίκαιον ὑπὲρ τῶν ἀδίκων,[5] τὸν ἄφθαρτον[6] ὑπὲρ τῶν φθαρτῶν,[7] τὸν ἀθάνατον[8] ὑπὲρ τῶν θνητῶν.[9] 3 τί γὰρ ἄλλο τὰς ἁμαρτίας ἡμῶν ἠδυνήθη καλύψαι[10] ἢ ἐκείνου δικαιοσύνη; 4 ἐν τίνι δικαιωθῆναι δυνατὸν τοὺς ἀνόμους[11] ἡμᾶς καὶ ἀσεβεῖς[12] ἢ ἐν μόνῳ τῷ υἱῷ τοῦ Θεοῦ; 5 ὦ[13] τῆς γλυκείας[14] ἀνταλλαγῆς,[15] ὦ[16] τῆς ἀνεξιχνιάστου[17] δημιουργίας,[18] ὦ[19] τῶν ἀπροσδοκήτων[20] εὐεργεσιῶν·[21] ἵνα ἀνομία[22] μὲν πολλῶν ἐν δικαίῳ ἑνὶ κρυβῇ,[23] δικαιοσύνη δὲ ἑνὸς πολλοὺς ἀνόμους[24] δικαιώσῃ. 6 ἐλέγξας[25] οὖν ἐν μὲν τῷ πρόσθεν[26] χρόνῳ τὸ ἀδύνατον[27] τῆς ἡμετέρας[28] φύσεως[29] εἰς τὸ τυχεῖν[30] ζωῆς, νῦν δὲ τὸν σωτῆρα[31] δείξας δυνατὸν σῴζειν καὶ τὰ ἀδύνατα,[32] ἐξ ἀμφοτέρων[33] ἐβουλήθη πιστεύειν ἡμᾶς τῇ

---

[1] ἀναδέχομαι aor mid ind 3s, accept, welcome

[2] λύτρον, ου, τό, price of release, ransom

[3] ἄνομος, ον, lawless, outside law

[4] ἄκακος, ον, innocent, guileless

[5] ἄδικος, ον, unjust, crooked

[6] ἄφθαρτος, ον, imperishable, incorruptible

[7] φθαρτός, όν, perishable

[8] ἀθάνατος, ον, immortal

[9] θνητός, ή, όν, mortal

[10] καλύπτω aor act inf, cover someone (up)

[11] ἄνομος, ον, lawless, outside law

[12] ἀσεβής, ές, irreverent, ungodly

[13] ὦ, interj, O, How!

[14] γλυκύς, εῖα, ύ sweet

[15] ἀνταλλαγή, ῆς, ἡ, exchange

[16] ὦ, interj, O, How!

[17] ἀνεξιχνίαστος, ον, inscrutable, incomprehensible

[18] δημιουργία, ας, ἡ, creative act

[19] ὦ, interj, O, How!

[20] ἀπροσδόκητος, ον, unexpected

[21] εὐεργεσία, ας, ἡ, doing of good, service

[22] ἀνομία, ας, ἡ, lawlessness

[23] κρύπτω aor pass sub 3s, hide, conceal

[24] ἄνομος, ον, lawless, outside law

[25] ἐλέγχω aor act ptcp m.s.nom., bring to light, expose

[26] πρόσθεν, adv, earlier, former

[27] ἀδύνατος, ον, powerless impossible

[28] ἡμέτερος, α, ον, our

[29] φῦσις, εως, ἡ, natural

[30] τυγχάνω aor act inf, meet, attain, gain, find, experience

[31] σωτήρ, ῆρος, ὁ, savior, deliverer, preserver

[32] ἀδύνατος, ον, powerless, impotent, impossible

[33] ἀμφότεροι, αι, α, both, all

χρηστότητι[1] αὐτοῦ, αὐτὸν ἡγεῖσθαι[2] τροφέα,[3] πατέρα, διδάσκαλον, σύμβουλον,[4] ἰατρόν,[5] νοῦν,[6] φῶς, τιμήν, δόξαν, ἰσχύν,[7] ζωήν.

10:1 Ταύτην καὶ σὺ τὴν πίστιν ἐὰν ποθήσῃς,[8] κατάλαβε[9] πρῶτον μὲν ἐπίγνωσιν[10] πατρός. **2** ὁ γὰρ Θεὸς τοὺς ἀνθρώπους ἠγάπησε, δι' οὓς ἐποίησε τὸν κόσμον, οἷς ὑπέταξε πάντα τὰ ἐν τῇ γῇ, οἷς λόγον ἔδωκεν, οἷς νοῦν,[11] οἷς μόνοις ἄνω[12] πρὸς οὐρανὸν ὁρᾶν ἐπέτρεψεν,[13] οὓς ἐκ τῆς ἰδίας εἰκόνος[14] ἔπλασε,[15] πρὸς οὓς ἀπέστειλε τὸν υἱὸν αὐτοῦ τὸν μονογενῆ,[16] οἷς τὴν ἐν οὐρανῷ βασιλείαν ἐπηγγείλατο[17] καὶ δώσει τοῖς ἀγαπήσασιν αὐτόν. **3** ἐπιγνοὺς δέ, τίνος οἴει[18] πληρωθήσεσθαι χαρᾶς; ἢ πῶς ἀγαπήσεις τὸν οὕτως προαγαπήσαντά[19] σε; **4** ἀγαπήσας δὲ μιμητὴς[20] ἔσῃ αὐτοῦ τῆς χρηστότητος.[21] καὶ μὴ θαυμάσῃς εἰ δύναται μιμητὴς[22] ἄνθρωπος γενέσθαι Θεοῦ· δύναται θέλοντος

---

[1] χρηστότης, ητος, ἡ, uprightness, goodness
[2] ἡγέομαι pres mid/pass inf, lead, guide, think
[3] τροφεύς, έως, ὁ, nourisher
[4] σύμβουλος, ου, ὁ, adviser, counsellor
[5] ἰατρός, οῦ, ὁ, physician
[6] νοῦς, νοός, νοΐ, νοῦν, ὁ, mind, intellect
[7] ἰσχύς, ύος, ἡ, strength, power
[8] ποθέω aor act sub 2s, desire, wish
[9] καταλαμβάνω aor act impv 2s, win, attain
[10] ἐπίγνωσις, εως, ἡ, knowledge, recognition
[11] νοῦς, νοός, νοΐ, νοῦν, ὁ, mind, intellect

[12] ἄνω, adv, above, upward(s), up
[13] ἐπιτρέπω aor act ind 3s, allow, permit
[14] εἰκών, όνος, ἡ, likeness, portrait
[15] πλάσσω aor act ind 3s, form, mold, shape
[16] μονογενής, ές, one and only, unique (in kind)
[17] ἐπαγγέλλω aor mid ind 3s, tell, proclaim, announce
[18] οἴομαι pres mid/pass ind 2s, think, suppose
[19] προαγαπάω aor act ptcp m.s.acc., love before, love first
[20] μιμητής, οῦ, ὁ, imitator
[21] χρηστότης, ητος, ἡ, uprightness, goodness
[22] μιμητής, οῦ, ὁ, imitator

αὐτοῦ. **5** οὐ γὰρ τὸ καταδυναστεύειν[1] τῶν πλησίον[2] οὐδὲ τὸ πλέον ἔχειν βούλεσθαι τῶν ἀσθενεστέρων[3] οὐδὲ τὸ πλουτεῖν[4] καὶ βιάζεσθαι[5] τοὺς ὑποδεεστέρους[6] εὐδαιμονεῖν[7] ἐστίν, οὐδὲ ἐν τούτοις δύναταί τις μιμήσασθαι[8] Θεόν, ἀλλὰ ταῦτα ἐκτὸς[9] τῆς ἐκείνου μεγαλειότητος.[10] **6** ἀλλ᾽ ὅστις τὸ τοῦ πλησίον[11] ἀναδέχεται[12] βάρος,[13] ὃς ἐν ᾧ κρείσσων[14] ἐστὶν ἕτερον τὸν ἐλαττούμενον[15] εὐεργετεῖν[16] ἐθέλει, ὃς ἃ παρὰ τοῦ Θεοῦ λαβὼν ἔχει, ταῦτα τοῖς ἐπιδεομένοις[17] χορηγῶν,[18] Θεὸς γίνεται τῶν λαμβανόντων, οὗτος μιμητής[19] ἐστι Θεοῦ. **7** τότε θεάσῃ[20] τυγχάνων[21] ἐπὶ γῆς ὅτι Θεὸς ἐν οὐρανοῖς πολιτεύεται,[22] τότε μυστήρια[23] Θεοῦ λαλεῖν ἄρξῃ, τότε τοὺς κολαζομένους[24] ἐπὶ τῷ μὴ θέλει ἀρνήσασθαι Θεὸν καὶ ἀγαπήσεις καὶ θαυμάσεις, τότε

---

[1] καταδυναστεύω pres act inf, oppress, exploit

[2] πλησίον, adv, near, close, neighbor

[3] ἀσθενής, ές, sick, ill, weak

[4] πλουτέω pres act inf, be rich

[5] βιάζω pres mid/pass inf, dominate, constrain

[6] ὑποδεής, ές, inferior, subservient

[7] εὐδαιμονέω pres act inf, be happy, fortunate

[8] μιμέομαι aor mid inf, imitate, emulate

[9] ἐκτός, impr prep, the outside, except

[10] μεγαλειότης, ητος, ἡ, grandeur, sublimity

[11] πλησίον, adv, near, close, neighbor

[12] ἀναδέχομαι pres mid/pass ind 3s, accept, receive, welcome

[13] βάρος, ους, τό, burden, claim of importance, fullness

[14] κρείττων, ον, prominent, higher in rank

[15] ἐλασσόω pres mid/pass ptcp m.s.acc., make lower, inferior

[16] εὐεργετέω pres act inf, do good to, benefit

[17] ἐπιδέομαι pres mid/pass ptcp m.p.dat., need, be in need

[18] χορηγέω pres act ptcp m.s.nom., provide, supply (in abundance)

[19] μιμητής, οῦ, ὁ, imitator

[20] θεάομαι fut mid ind 2s, see, look at

[21] τυγχάνω pres act ptcp m.s.nom., meet, attain

[22] πολιτεύομαι pres mid/pass ind 3s, have one's citizenship

[23] μυστήριον, ου, τό, (God's) secret, transcendent/ultimate reality

[24] κολάζω pres mid/pass ptcp m.p.acc., penalize, punish

τῆς ἀπάτης[1] τοῦ κόσμου καὶ τῆς πλάνης[2] καταγνώσῃ,[3] ὅταν τὸ ἀληθῶς[4] ἐν οὐρανῷ ζῆν ἐπιγνῷς, ὅταν τοῦ δοκοῦντος ἐνθάδε[5] θανάτου καταφρονήσῃς,[6] ὅταν τὸν ὄντως[7] θάνατον φοβηθῇς, ὃς φυλάσσεται τοῖς κατακριθησομένοις[8] εἰς τὸ πῦρ τὸ αἰώνιον, ὃ τοὺς παραδοθέντας αὐτῷ μέχρι[9] τέλους κολάσει.[10] **8** τότε τοὺς ὑπομένοντας[11] ὑπὲρ δικαιοσύνης θαυμάσεις τὸ πῦρ τὸ πρόσκαιρον,[12] καὶ μακαρίσεις,[13] ὅταν ἐκεῖνο τὸ πῦρ ἐπιγνῷς.

11:1 Οὐ ξένα [14]ὁμιλῶ[15] οὐδὲ παραλόγως[16] ζητῶ, ἀλλὰ στόλων γενόμενος μαθητὴς γίνομαι διδάσκαλος ἐθνῶν· τὰ παραδοθέντα ἀξίως[17] ὑπηρετῶν[18] γινομένοις ἀληθείας μαθηταῖς. **2** τίς γὰρ ὀρθῶς[19] διδαχθεὶς καὶ λόγῳ[20] προσφιλὴς[21] γενηθεὶς οὐκ ἐπιζητεῖ[22] σαφῶς[23] μαθεῖν[24] τὰ διὰ Λόγου[25] δειχθέντα φανερῶς[26] μαθηταῖς; οἷς ἐφανέρωσεν ὁ Λόγος[27] φανείς,

---

[1] ἀπάτη, ης, ἡ, deception, deceitfulness

[2] πλάνη, ης, ἡ, error, delusion

[3] καταγινώσκω fut mid ind 2s, condemn, convict

[4] ἀληθῶς, adv, truly, actually

[5] ἐνθάδε, adv, here

[6] καταφρονέω aor act sub 2s, look down on, despise

[7] ὄντως, adv, really, certainly

[8] κατακρίνω fut pass ptcp m.p.dat., pronounce a sentence on

[9] μέχρι, impr prep, as far as, until

[10] κόλασις, εως, ἡ, punishment

[11] ὑπομένω pres act ptcp m.p.acc., remain/stay (behind), hold out, endure

[12] πρόσκαιρος, ον, temporary, transitory

[13] μακαρίζω fut act ind 2s, call/consider blessed, happy

[14] ξένος, η, ον, strange, alien

[15] ὁμιλέω pres act ind 1s, speak, address

[16] παραλόγως, adv, in an unreasonable manner

[17] ἀξίως, adv, worthily

[18] ὑπηρετέω pres act ptcp m.s.nom., serve, be helpful

[19] ὀρθῶς, adv, rightly, correctly

[20] Λόγος, ου, ὁ, word, the Logos

[21] προσφιλής, ές, pleasing, agreeable

[22] ἐπιζητέω pres act ind 3s, search for

[23] σαφῶς, adv, clearly, exactly

[24] μανθάνω aor act inf, learn

[25] Λόγος, ου, ὁ, word, the Logos

[26] φανερῶς, adv, openly, publicly

[27] Λόγος, ου, ὁ, word, the Logos

παρρησίᾳ λαλῶν, ὑπὸ ἀπίστων[1] μὴ νοούμενος,[2] μαθηταῖς δὲ διηγούμενος,[3] οἳ πιστοὶ λογισθέντες ὑπ' αὐτοῦ ἔγνωσαν πατρὸς μυστήρια.[4] **3** οὗ χάριν[5] ἀπέστειλε Λόγον,[6] ἵνα κόσμῳ φανῇ, ὃς ὑπὸ λαοῦ ἀτιμασθείς,[7] διὰ ἀποστόλων κηρυχθείς, ὑπὸ ἐθνῶν ἐπιστεύθη. **4** οὗτος ὁ ἀπ' ἀρχῆς, ὁ καινὸς φανεὶς καὶ παλαιὸς[8] εὑρεθεὶς καὶ πάντοτε νέος[9] ἐν ἁγίων καρδίαις γεννώμενος. **5** οὗτος ὁ ἀεί,[10] ὁ σήμερον υἱὸς λογισθείς, δι' οὗ πλουτίζεται[11] ἡ ἐκκλησία καὶ χάρις ἁπλουμένη[12] ἐν ἁγίοις πληθύνεται,[13] παρέχουσα[14] νοῦν,[15] φανεροῦσα μυστήρια,[16] διαγγέλλουσα[17] καιρούς, χαίρουσα ἐπὶ πιστοῖς, ἐπιζητοῦσι[18] δωρουμένη,[19] οἷς ὅρκια.[20] πίστεως οὐ θραύεται[21] οὐδὲ ὅρια[22] πατέρων παρορίζεται.[23] **6** εἶτα[24] φόβος νόμου ᾄδεται[25] καὶ προφητῶν χάρις γινώσκεται καὶ εὐαγγελίων πίστις ἵδρυται[26] καὶ ἀποστόλων παράδοσις[27] φυλάσσεται καὶ ἐκκλησίας χαρὰ

---

[1] ἄπιστος, ον, unbelievable

[2] νοέω pres mid/pass ptcp m.s.nom., perceive

[3] διηγέομαι pres mid/pass ptcp m.s.nom., tell, relate, describe

[4] μυστήριον, ου, τό, (God's) secret, transcendent/ultimate reality

[5] χάριν, impr prep, for the sake of, on behalf of

[6] Λόγος, ου, ὁ, word, the Logos

[7] ἀτιμάζω aor pass ptcp m.s.nom., dishonor/shame

[8] παλαιός, ά, όν, old, obsolete

[9] νέος, α, ον, new, young, novice

[10] ἀεί, adv, always, continually

[11] πλουτίζω pres mid/pass ind 3s, make wealthy, make rich

[12] ἁπλόω pres mid/pass ptcp f.s.nom., make single, unfold

[13] πληθύνω pres mid/pass ind 3s, increase, multiply

[14] παρέχω pres act ptcp f.s.nom., give up, offer

[15] νοῦς, νοός, νοΐ, νοῦν, ὁ, mind

[16] μυστήριον, ου, τό, (God's) secret, transcendent/ultimate reality

[17] διαγγέλλω pres act ptcp f.s.nom., proclaim

[18] ἐπιζητέω pres act ptcp m.p.dat., search for

[19] δωρέω pres mid/pass ptcp f.s.nom., give, present

[20] ὅρκιον, ου, τό, oath, vow, pledge

[21] θραύω pres mid/pass ind 3s, break, weaken, oppress

[22] ὅριον, ου, τό, boundary

[23] παρορίζω pres mid/pass ind 3s, overstep, transgress

[24] εἶτα, adv, then, next, furthermore

[25] ᾄδω pres mid/pass ind 3s, sing (in praise)

[26] ἱδρύω pres mid/pass ind 3s, be seated, be established

[27] παράδοσις, εως, ἡ, surrender, arrest, tradition

σκιρτᾷ.¹ **7** ἣν χάριν μὴ λυπῶν² ἐπιγνώσῃ ἃ Λόγος³ ὁμιλεῖ⁴ δι' ὧν βούλεται, ὅτε θέλει. **8** ὅσα γὰρ θελήματι τοῦ κελεύοντος⁵ Λόγου⁶ ἐκινήθημεν⁷ ἐξειπεῖν⁸ μετὰ πόνου,⁹ ἐξ ἀγάπης τῶν ἀποκαλυφθέντων¹⁰ ἡμῖν γινόμεθα ὑμῖν κοινωνοί.¹¹

12:1 Οἷς ἐντυχόντες¹² καὶ ἀκούσαντες μετὰ σπουδῆς¹³ εἴσεσθε ὅσα παρέχει¹⁴ ὁ Θεὸς τοῖς ἀγαπῶσιν ὀρθῶς,¹⁵ οἱ γενόμενοι παράδεισος¹⁶ τρυφῆς,¹⁷ πάγκαρπον¹⁸ ξύλον,¹⁹ εὐθαλοῦν,²⁰ ἀνατείλαντες²¹ ἐν ἑαυτοῖς, ποικίλοις²² καρποῖς κεκοσμημένοι.²³ **2** ἐν γὰρ τούτῳ τῷ χωρίῳ²⁴ ξύλον²⁵ γνώσεως²⁶ καὶ ξύλον²⁷ ζωῆς πεφύτευται·²⁸ ἀλλ' οὐ τὸ τῆς γνώσεως²⁹ ἀναιρεῖ,³⁰ ἀλλ' ἡ παρακοὴ³¹ ἀναιρεῖ.³² **3** οὐδὲ γὰρ ἄσημα³³ τὰ γεγραμμένα, ὡς Θεὸς

---

¹ σκιρτάω pres act ind 3s, leap, spring about
² λυπέω pres act ptcp m.s.nom., vex
³ Λόγος, ου, ὁ, word, the Logos
⁴ ὁμιλέω pres act ind 3s, speak, address
⁵ κελεύω pres act ptcp m.s.gen., command, order, urge
⁶ Λόγος, ου, ὁ, word, the Logos
⁷ κινέω aor pass ind 1p, move away, set in motion
⁸ ἐξαγορεύω aor act inf, express
⁹ πόνος, ου, ὁ, (hard) labor, toil
¹⁰ ἀποκαλύπτω aor pass ptcp n.p.gen., reveal
¹¹ κοινωνός, οῦ, ὁ/ἡ, companion, sharer
¹² ἐντυγχάνω aor act ptcp m.p.nom., approach, appeal
¹³ σπουδή, ης, ἡ, haste, speed, eagerness
¹⁴ παρέχω pres act ind 3s, give up, offer, present
¹⁵ ὀρθῶς, adv, rightly, correctly
¹⁶ παράδεισος, ου, ὁ, paradise
¹⁷ τρυφή, ῆς, ἡ, indulgence
¹⁸ πάγκαρπος, ον, bearing much fruit
¹⁹ ξύλον, ου, τό, wood, tree
²⁰ εὐθαλέω pres act ptcp n.s.nom., flourish, thrive
²¹ ἀνατέλλω aor act ptcp m.p.nom., rise
²² ποικίλος, η, ον, diversified
²³ κοσμέω perf mid/pass ptcp m.p.nom., make neat
²⁴ χωρίον, ου, τό, place, piece of land, field, (a city and its) environs
²⁵ ξύλον, ου, τό, wood, tree
²⁶ γνῶσις, εως, ἡ, knowledge
²⁷ ξύλον, ου, τό, wood, tree
²⁸ φυτεύω perf mid/pass ind 3s, plant
²⁹ γνῶσις, εως, ἡ, knowledge
³⁰ ἀναιρέω pres act ind 3s, take away
³¹ παρακοή, ῆς, ἡ, disobedience
³² ἀναιρέω pres act ind 3s, take away
³³ ἄσημος, ον, insignificant

ἀπ᾽ ἀρχῆς ξύλον¹ γνώσεως² καὶ ξύλον³ ζωῆς ἐν μέσῳ παραδείσου⁴
ἐφύτευσε,⁵ διὰ γνώσεως⁶ ζωὴν ἐπιδεικνύς·⁷ ᾗ μὴ καθαρῶς⁸ χρη-
σάμενοι⁹ οἱ ἀπ᾽ ἀρχῆς πλάνῃ¹⁰ τοῦ ὄφεως¹¹ γεγύμνωνται.¹² **4** οὐδὲ
γὰρ ζωὴ ἄνευ¹³ γνώσεως,¹⁴ οὐδὲ γνῶσις¹⁵ ἀσφαλὴς¹⁶ ἄνευ¹⁷ ζωῆς
ἀληθοῦς·¹⁸ διὸ πλησίον¹⁹ ἑκάτερον²⁰ πεφύτευται.²¹ **5** ἣν δύναμιν
ἐνιδὼν²² ὁ ἀπόστολος τήν τε ἄνευ²³ ἀληθείας προστάγματος²⁴
εἰς ζωὴν ἀσκουμένην²⁵ γνῶσιν²⁶ μεμφόμενος²⁷ λέγει· Ἡ γνῶσις²⁸
φυσιοῖ,²⁹ ἡ δὲ ἀγάπη οἰκοδομεῖ. **6** ὁ γὰρ νομίζων³⁰ εἰδέναι τι
ἄνευ³¹ γνώσεως³² ἀληθοῦς³³ καὶ μαρτυρουμένης ὑπὸ τῆς ζωῆς,
οὐκ ἔγνω· ὑπὸ τοῦ ὄφεως³⁴ πλανᾶται, μὴ ἀγαπήσας τὸ ζῆν. ὁ δὲ
μετὰ φόβου ἐπιγνοὺς καὶ ζωὴν ἐπιζητῶν³⁵ ἐπ᾽ ἐλπίδι φυτεύει,³⁶

---

¹ ξύλον, ου, τό, wood, tree
² γνῶσις, εως, ἡ, knowledge
³ ξύλον, ου, τό, wood, tree
⁴ παράδεισος, ου, ὁ, paradise
⁵ φυτεύω aor act ind 3s, plant
⁶ γνῶσις, εως, ἡ, knowledge
⁷ ἐπιδείκνυμι pres act ptcp
  m.s.nom., show, point out
⁸ καθαρῶς, adv, in purity
⁹ χράομαι aor mid ptcp m.p.nom.,
  employ
¹⁰ πλάνη, ης, ἡ, error, delusion
¹¹ ὄφις, εως, ἡ, snake, serpent
¹² γυμνόω perf mid/pass ind 3p,
  strip, lay bare
¹³ ἄνευ, prep, without
¹⁴ γνῶσις, εως, ἡ, knowledge
¹⁵ γνῶσις, εως, ἡ, knowledge
¹⁶ ἀσφαλής, ές, firm, certain
¹⁷ ἄνευ, prep, without
¹⁸ ἀληθής, ές, truthful, honest, true
¹⁹ πλησίον, α, ον, nearby, near,
  neighbor
²⁰ ἑκάτερος, α, ον, each of two,
  both

²¹ φυτεύω perf mid/pass ind 3s,
  plant
²² ἐνοράω aor act ptcp m.s.nom., see,
  perceive
²³ ἄνευ, prep, without
²⁴ πρόσταγμα, ατος, τό,
  command(ment), injunction
²⁵ ἀσκέω pres mid/pass ptcp f.s.acc.,
  practice, engage in
²⁶ γνῶσις, εως, ἡ, knowledge
²⁷ μέμφομαι pres mid/pass ptcp
  m.s.nom., find fault with, blame
²⁸ γνῶσις, εως, ἡ, knowledge
²⁹ φυσιόω pres act ind 3s, puff up,
  make proud
³⁰ νομίζω pres act ptcp m.s.nom.,
  think, consider
³¹ ἄνευ, prep, without
³² γνῶσις, εως, ἡ, knowledge, what
  is known
³³ ἀληθής, ές, truthful, honest, true
³⁴ ὄφις, εως, ἡ, snake, serpent
³⁵ ἐπιζητέω pres act ptcp m.s.nom.,
  search for, seek after
³⁶ φυτεύω pres act ind 3s, plant

καρπὸνπροσδοκῶν.[1] **7** ἤτω σοι καρδία γνῶσις,[2] ζωὴ δὲ λόγος ἀληθής,[3] χωρούμενος.[4] **8** οὗ ξύλον[5] φέρων καὶ καρπὸν αἴρων[6] τρυγήσεις[7] ἀεὶ[8] τὰ παρὰ Θεῷ ποθούμενα,[9] ὧν ὄφις[10] οὐχ ἅπτεται οὐδὲ πλάνη[11] συγχρωτίζεται·[12] οὐδὲ Εὕα[13] φθείρεται,[14] ἀλλὰ παρθένος[15] πιστεύεται. **9** καὶ σωτήριον[16] δείκνυται, καὶ ἀπόστολοι συνετίζονται,[17] καὶ τὸ Κυρίου πάσχα[18] προέρχεται,[19] καὶ κλῆροι[20] συνάγονται καὶ πάντα μετὰ κόσμου ἁρμόζεται,[21] καὶ διδάσκων ἁγίους ὁ Λόγος[22] εὐφραίνεται,[23] δι' οὗ Πατὴρ δοξάζεται· ᾧ ἡ δόξα εἰς τοὺς αἰῶνας. Ἀμήν.

---

[1] προσδοκάω pres act ptcp m.s.nom., wait for, look for

[2] γνῶσις, εως, ἡ, knowledge

[3] ἀληθής, ές, truthful, true

[4] χωρέω pres mid/pass ptcp m.s.nom., go, go out/away

[5] ξύλον, ου, τό, wood, tree

[6] αἱρέω pres act ptcp m.s.nom., lift up

[7] τρυγάω fut act ind 2s, harvest grapes

[8] ἀεί, adv, always, continually

[9] ποθέω pres mid/pass ptcp n.p.acc., desire, wish (for)

[10] ὄφις, εως, ἡ, snake, serpent

[11] πλάνη, ης, ἡ, error, delusion

[12] συγχρωτίζομαι pres mid/pass ind 3s, defile by touching

[13] Εὕα, ας, ἡ, Eve

[14] φθείρω pres mid/pass ind 3s, destroy

[15] παρθένος, ου, ἡ, virgin, chaste person

[16] σωτήριον, ου, τό, deliverance, salvation

[17] συνετίζω pres mid/pass ind 3p, cause to understand

[18] πάσχα, τό, the Passover

[19] προέρχομαι pres mid/pass ind 3s, go forward

[20] κλῆρος, ου, ὁ, lot, portion

[21] ἁρμόζω pres mid/pass ind 3s, fit, join

[22] Λόγος, ου, ὁ, word, the Logos

[23] εὐφραίνω pres mid/pass ind 3s, gladden

ADDITIONAL RESOURCES FOR FURTHER STUDY

Polycarp to the Philippians Beginning

Dehandschutter, Boudewijn. "The Epistle of Polycarp." In *Apostolic Fathers: An Introduction*, edited by Wilhelm Pratscher, translated by Elisabeth G. Wolfe, 117–29. Waco, TX: Baylor University Press, 2010.

Hartog, Paul A. "The Opponents of Polycarp, *Philippians*, and 1 John." In *Trajectories through the New Testament and the Apostolic Fathers*, vol. 2 of *The New Testament and the Apostolic Fathers*, edited by Andrew Gregory and Christopher Tuckett, 375–91. Oxford: Oxford University Press, 2005.

Holmes, Michael. "Polycarp of Smyrna, Letter to the Philippians." In *The Writings of the Apostolic Fathers*, edited by Paul Foster, 108–25. London: T&T Clark, 2007.

Oakes, Peter. "Leadership and Suffering in the Letters of Polycarp and Paul to the Philippians." In *Trajectories through the New Testament and the Apostolic Fathers*, vol. 2 of *The New Testament and the Apostolic Fathers*, edited by Andrew Gregory and Christopher Tuckett, 353–73. Oxford: Oxford University Press, 2005.

Polycarp to the Philippians Intermediate

Berding, Kenneth Andrew. "Polycarp of Smyrna's View of the Authorship of 1 and 2 Timothy." *VC* 53.4 (1999): 349–60.

Hartog, Paul A. *Polycarp and the New Testament: The Occasion, Rhetoric, Theme, and Unity of the Epistle to the Philippians and Its Allusions to New Testament Literature.* WUNT 2/134. Tübingen: Mohr Siebeck, 2002.

———. *Polycarp's Epistle to the Philippians and the Martyrdom of Polycarp: Introduction, Text, and Commentary.* Oxford Apostolic Fathers. Oxford: Oxford University Press, 2013.

Hill, Charles E. *From the Lost Teaching of Polycarp: Identifying Irenaeus' Apostolic Presbyter and the Author of* Ad Diognetum. WUNT 186. Tübingen: Mohr Siebeck, 2006.

Holmes, Michael. "Polycarp's *Letter to the Philippians* and the Writings That Later Formed the New Testament." In *The Reception of the New Testament in the Apostolic Fathers*, vol. 1 of *The New Testament and the Apostolic Fathers*, edited by Andrew Gregory and Christopher Tuckett, 187–227. Oxford: Oxford University Press, 2005.

Maier, Harry. "Purity and Danger in Polycarp's Epistle to the Philippians: The Sin of Valens in Social Perspective." *JECS* 1.3 (1993): 229–47.

Polycarp to the Philippians Advanced

Bauer, J. B. *Die Polykarpbriefe*. KAV 5. Göttingen: Vandenhoeck und Ruprecht, 1995.

Berding, Kenneth Andrew. *Polycarp and Paul: An Analysis of Their Literary and Theological Relationship in Light of Polycarp's Use of Biblical and Extra-Biblical Literature*. VCSup 62. Leiden: Brill, 2002.

Dehandschutter, Boudewijn. *Polycarpiana. Studies on Martyrdom and Persecution in Early Christianity: Collected Essays*. BETL 205. Leuven: Leuven University Press, 2007.

Schoedel, William R. "Polycarp of Smyrna and Ignatius of Antioch." In *ANRW* 2.27.1, edited by Wolfgang Haase, 272–358. Berlin: de Gruyter, 1993.

———. "Polycarp's Witness to Ignatius of Antioch." *VC* 41.1 (1987): 1–10.

Martyrdom of Polycarp Beginning

Buschmann, Gerd. "The Martyrdom of Polycarp." In *Apostolic Fathers: An Introduction*, edited by Wilhelm Pratscher, translated by Elisabeth G. Wolfe, 135–53. Waco, TX: Baylor University Press, 2010.

Dehandschutter, B. "The New Testament and the *Martyrdom of Polycarp*." In *Trajectories through the New Testament and the Apostolic Fathers*, vol. 2 of *The New Testament and the Apostolic Fathers*, edited by Andrew Gregory and Christopher Tuckett, 395–405. Oxford: Oxford University Press, 2005.

Holmes, Michael. "The *Martyrdom of Polycarp* and the New Testament Passion Narratives." In *Trajectories through the New Testament and the Apostolic Fathers*, vol. 2 of *The New Testament and the Apostolic Fathers*, edited by Andrew Gregory and Christopher Tuckett, 407–32. Oxford: Oxford University Press, 2005.

Parvis, Sara. "The Martyrdom of Polycarp." In *The Writings of the Apostolic Fathers*, edited by Paul Foster, 126–46. London: T&T Clark, 2007.

Wilhite, Shawn J. "That We Too Might Be Imitators of Him': The Martyrdom of Polycarp as *Imitatio Christi*." *Churchman* 129.4 (Winter 2015): 319–36.

Martyrdom of Polycarp Intermediate

Cobb, L. Stephanie. "Polycarp's Cup: Imitatio in the Martyrdom of Polycarp." *Journal of Religious History* 38.2 (2014): 224–40.

Dehandschutter, Boudewijn. "The Martyrium Polycarpi: A Century of Research." In *ANRW* 2.27.1, edited by Wolfgang Haase, 485–522. Berlin and New York: de Gruyter, 1993.

Gibson, E Leigh. "The Jews and Christians in the Martyrdom of Polycarp: Entangled or Parted Ways?" In *The Ways That Never Parted: Jews and Christians in Late Antiquity and the Early Middle Ages*, edited by Adam H. Becker and Annette Yoshiko Reed, 145–58. Tübingen: Mohr Siebeck, 2003.

Hartog, Paul A. "The Christology of the Martyrdom of Polycarp: Martyrdom as Both Imitation of Christ and Election by Christ." *Perichoresis* 12.2 (2014): 137–52.

————. *Polycarp's Epistle to the Philippians and the Martyrdom of Polycarp: Introduction, Text, and Commentary*. Oxford Apostolic Fathers. Oxford: Oxford University Press, 2013.

Moss, Candida R. "Nailing Down and Tying Up: Lessons in Intertextual Impossibility from the Martyrdom of Polycarp." *VC* 67.2 (2013): 117–36.

Martyrdom of Polycarp Advanced

Buschmann, Gerd. *Das Martyrium Des Polykarp*. KAV 6. Göttingen: Vandenhoeck & Ruprecht, 1998.

Dehandschutter, B. *Polycarpiana. Studies on Martyrdom and Persecution in Early Christianity: Collected Essays*. BETL 205. Leuven: Leuven University Press, 2007.

Hoover, Jesse. "False Lives, False Martyrs: 'Pseudo-Pionius' and the Redating of the Martyrdom of Polycarp." *VC* 67.5 (2013): 471–98.

Khomych, Taras. "The Martyrdom of Polycarp in Church Slavonic: An Evidence of the Academic Menologion." *VC* 67. 4 (2013): 393–406.

Moss, Candida R. *Ancient Christian Martyrdom: Diverse Practices, Theologies, and Traditions*. New Haven: Yale University Press, 2012.

————. "On the Dating of Polycarp: Rethinking the Place of the Martyrdom of Polycarp in the History of Christianity." *EC* 1.4 (2010): 539–74.

Fragments of Papias Beginning

Bauckham, Richard. *Jesus and the Eyewitnesses: The Gospels as Eyewitness Testimony*. Grand Rapids: Eerdmans, 2006.

Hill, Charles E. "The Fragments of Papias." In *The Writings of the Apostolic Fathers*, edited by Paul Foster, 42–51. London: T&T Clark, 2007.

Tasmuth, Randar. "Authority, Authorship, and Apostolicity as a Part of the Johannine Question: The Role of Papias in the Search for the Authoritative Author of the Gospel of John." *Concordia* 33.1 (2007): 26–42.

Yarbrough, Robert W. "The Date of Papias: A Reassessment." *JETS* 26.2 (1983): 181–91.

Fragments of Papias Intermediate

Bauckham, Richard. "Papias and Polycrates on the Origin of the Fourth Gospel." *JTS* 44.1 (1993): 24–69.

Hill, Charles E. "What Papias Said About John (and Luke): A 'New' Papian Fragment." *JTS* 49.2 (1998): 582–629.

Hughes, Kyle R. "The Lukan Special Material and the Tradition History of the Pericope Adulterae." *NovT* 55.3 (2013): 232–51.

Manor, T. Scott. "Papias, Origen, and Eusebius: The Criticisms and Defense of the Gospel of John." *VC* 67.1 (2013): 1–21.

Shanks, Monte A. *Papias and the New Testament*. Eugene, OR: Wipf and Stock, 2013.

Fragments of Papias Advanced

Baum, Armin Daniel. "Papias als Kommentator evangelischer Aussprüche Jesu: Erwägungen zur Art seines Werkes." *NovT* 38.3 (1996): 257–76.

Black, Matthew. "The Use of Rhetorical Terminology in Papias on Mark and Matthew." *JSNT* 37 (1989): 31–41.

Körtner, Ulrich and Martin Leutzsch. *Schriften des Urchristentums. Teil 3: Papiasfragmente. Hirt des Hermas. Eingeleitet, herausgegeben, übertragen und erläutert.* Darmstadt: Wissenschaftliche Buchgesellschaft, 1998.

MacDonald, Dennis Ronald. *Two Shipwrecked Gospels: The Logoi of Jesus and Papias's Exposition of Logia about the Lord.* Early Christianity and Its Literature 8. Atlanta, GA: Society of Biblical Literature, 2012.

Schoedel, William R. "Papias." In *ANRW* 2.27.1, edited by Wolfgang Haase, 235–70. Berlin: de Gruyter, 1993.

Letter to Diognetus Beginning

Costache, Doru. "Christianity and the World in the Letter to Diognetus: Inferences for Contemporary Ecclesial Experience." *Phronema* 27.1 (2012): 29–50.

Dunning, Benjamin H. *Aliens and Sojourners: Self as Other in Early Christianity.* Philadelphia, PA: University of Pennsylvania Press, 2009.

Foster, Paul. "The *Epistle to Diognetus*." In *The Writings of the Apostolic Fathers*, edited by Paul Foster, 147–56. London: T&T Clark, 2007.

Hollon, Bryan C. "Is the Epistle to Diognetus an Apology? A Rhetorical Analysis." *Journal of Communication and Religion* 29.1 (2006): 127–46.

Letter to Diognetus Intermediate

Bird, Michael F. "The Reception of Paul in the *Epistle to Diognetus*." Pages 70–90 in *Paul and the Second Century*, edited by Michael F. Bird and Joseph R. Dodson, 70–90. London: T&T Clark, 2011.

Crowe, Brandon D. "Oh Sweet Exchange! The Soteriological Significance of the Incarnation in the *Epistle to Diognetus*." *ZNW* 102.1 (2011): 96–109.

Hill, Charles E. *From the Lost Teaching of Polycarp: Identifying Irenaeus' Apostolic Presbyter and the Author of* Ad Diognetum. WUNT 186. Tübingen: Mohr Siebeck, 2006.

Jefford, Clayton N. *The Epistle to Diognetus (with the Fragment of Quadratus): Introduction, Text, and Commentary*. Oxford Apostolic Fathers. Oxford: Oxford University Press, 2013.

Perendy, László. "The Threads of Tradition: The Parallelisms between Ad Diognetum and Ad Autolycum." *Studia Patristica* 65 (2013): 197–207.

Reis, David Michael. "Thinking with Soul: Psyche and Psychikos in the Construction of Early Christian Identities." *JECS* 17.4 (2009): 563–603.

Letter to Diognetus Advanced

Baumeister, Theofried. "Zur Datierung der Schrift an Diognet." *Vigiliae Christianae* 42.2 (1988): 105–11.

Bourlet, Michel, Roland Minnerath, Marie-Hélène Congourdeau, and Xavier Morales, eds. *Apologie à Diognète. Exhortation aux Grecs.* Les Pères Dans La Foi 83. La Ferrière: Littéral, 2002.

Heintz, Michael. "Mimētēs Theou in the Epistle to Diognetus." *JECS* 12.1 (2004): 107–19.

Lona, Horacio. "Zur Struktur von Diog 5–6." *VC* 54.1 (2000): 32–43.

Rizzi, Marco. *"La questione dell'unità dell' 'Ad Diognetum'." Studia Patristica Mediolanensia* 16 (1989): 162–70.